From Prisoner to Professor

How the Angola Prison Revival Launched

an International Ministry

By Dr. Alex Hennis

Empoword Publishing Worldwide

17127 Wax Rd Bldg A

Greenwell Springs, LA 70739

www.EmpowordPublishing.com

(225) 412-3130

FROM PRISONER TO PROFESSOR by Dr. Alex Hennis

Published by Empoword Publishing Worldwide

Copyright © 2024 by Dr. Alex Hennis

From Prisoner to Professor: How the Angola Prison Revival Launched an International Ministry

by Dr. Alex Hennis

Endorsements

Alex Hennis has a passion for God. His story is a powerful one of redemption and restoration. You will be fascinated and blessed by this young man's story—I know I was.

Ruth Graham, Author of *"Forgiving Father, Forgiving Myself, An Invitation to the Miracle of Forgiveness"*

Having known Alex for more than a dozen years, I can verify the amazing work God has done in Alex's life. After earning his Doctor of Ministry degree while at Angola, Alex is now serving as a faculty member at Global University, and the influence of Alex's ministry has spread to the nations. A wonderful story of transformation and the grace of God in his life.

Dr. Gary Seevers, Ph.D., President of Global University

Dr. Alex Hennis, an authentic man of God, tells his compelling life story in these pages. Dr. Hennis has not only lived a unique life filled with adventure, danger, defeat, failure, and suffering, but he has also lived under the incredible grace of a loving God. It is hard to imagine a more compelling illustration of God's power, love, and mercy than the life of Dr. Hennis. This story is only the beginning, however, as God continues to build on this foundation a gifted ministry of worldwide service and impact.

Dr. Randy Hedlun, Th.D., Dean of Graduate Studies, Global University

In the transformative narrative of Alex Hennis' journey, readers are introduced to a man whose incarceration became the unlikely catalyst for profound education and spiritual growth. As an inmate in a Louisiana prison, Hennis' collaboration with a Chaplain—later Warden—proved pivotal. Together, they enriched the lives of many men through Associate Degree programs in education and religious studies. He also initiated a Church at the prison. Hennis' relentless pursuit of knowledge led him to attain three Master's degrees and a Doctorate, credentials that speak volumes to his dedication. His story is a testament to the power of hard work and the indomitable human spirit, as he played a crucial role in expanding educational opportunities behind bars, lighting a path of hope and redemption for many.

Dr. Wayne Cook T.h.D.

Warden, Chaplain, and Senior Pastor of Lakeside Presbyterian Church in Chapala, Mexico

It is exciting to see the in-depth story of a life-changing miracle. Alex's transformation is a testimony that will encourage, inspire, and move you with hope. God proves once again through Alex that no life is unreachable and no place we find ourselves is forgotten. God still sees and redeems.

Scott Holmes D.Min

District Superintendent of the Louisiana Assemblies of God

Over the past four decades, I've worked diligently to ensure public safety. In my professional career, I have not seen anything change lives like the gospel of Jesus Christ. This observation motivated me to establish Seminary programs in prisons across the country. Dr. Alex Hennis' life has been proof of their effectiveness. He worked to help better the Louisiana and Mississippi prison systems. Now, he's working to make the world a better place. From a prisoner to an international minister, he is "The Prison Seminary Poster Child.

Burl Cain Commissioner of the Mississippi Department of Corrections (Previous Warden of Angola) CEO of Prison Seminaries Foundation

I had the privilege of meeting Alex for the first time at the Parish Prison in Baton Rouge over forty years ago. Surprisingly, he was full of the Spirit of the Lord and desirous to reach the world with the gospel. At first, I thought that Alex would be released after his trial, and he would be free to preach the gospel. To our surprise, at his trial, the judge sentenced him to prison. As Alex was transferred throughout the system over the years, I kept in touch with him, visiting and mentoring him. He became like a son to me. One fateful day, I got to watch God deliver him from prison after a quarter of a century of incarceration. Now, I've had the privilege and joy of watching him fulfill that desire to reach the world with the gospel. Dr. Alex Hennis is now traveling the globe, winning the lost, training the found, and moving in signs and wonders.

Pastor Carl Everett

Assistant Pastor/Bethany and Founder of the Bethany Cell Church Network. Author of *Great is His Faithfulness*

Table of Contents

Introduction

In order to better appreciate a man's current circumstances, it's crucial to grasp his journey. If I were to share that I've attained two associate degrees, one bachelor's degree, three master's degrees, and a doctorate degree, all while maintaining an A average, won numerous rodeo championship buckles, and been featured in documentaries and various media outlets from the Boston Globe to the London Times, served as a missionary, established a church, and secured a job with a university, you might find it impressive. But what if I revealed that I accomplished all of this while incarcerated? It might leave you in disbelief, wouldn't it?

If you're willing to journey with me through the remaining pages, I'll recount the story of how I believe God granted me these opportunities within the Louisiana State Penitentiary, infamously known as Angola. I was fortunate to be part of the remarkable transformation of Angola from what was once deemed the bloodiest 18,000 acres of American real estate to a bastion of peace and stability. The prison underwent a remarkable shift from a place reminiscent of a medieval slave camp to a destination for tourists. Witnessing a revival of such magnitude was awe-inspiring. No single individual can claim sole responsibility for the profound change that transpired; it was nothing short of a miracle.

Have you ever wondered, "How does a young individual find themselves in prison?" Why would someone trade the freedom and protections guaranteed by the United States Constitution for a life behind bars? Why sacrifice the possibility of achieving the American dream for a living nightmare? The answers to these questions are intricate and vary from person to person. Perhaps by sharing my story, I can shed light on some of those answers and potentially provide healing for those who have made regrettable choices. Maybe it can inspire the average person to strive for greater heights, to achieve more, and to refuse to let circumstances determine whether they accomplish something significant. So, how does one end up in prison or achieve something noteworthy? In my view, it boils down to one choice at a time.

The overcrowded prison system in the United States stands as a stark reminder of the broken homes scattered across America. Undoubtedly, my upbringing played a significant role in shaping the path I walked and the decisions I made. However, I acknowledge full responsibility for those decisions. True progress and personal growth can only occur when one takes ownership of the consequences of their actions, rather than placing blame elsewhere. Moreover, dwelling on past pain, disappointment, and rejection should never serve as an excuse to stagnate in life. As the saying goes, "One cannot move forward while constantly looking in the rearview mirror."

Chapter 1

Where it all started

W

hen I was a baby, my father left my mother and me to fend for ourselves. He never made any effort to support us or establish a relationship with me. My mother worked tirelessly to ensure we had what we needed to get by. Frequently, she had to take on two jobs just to keep up with the bills and put food on the table. This challenging situation often left me alone at home. With no supervision, I eventually began wandering the neighborhood and falling in with the wrong crowd.

Reflecting on my life, a recurring pattern becomes apparent. I consistently gravitated towards undisciplined groups headed for trouble. Whenever our financial situation deteriorated, it inevitably led to my mother and me relocating. Each time, a new troubled crowd seemed poised to embrace me. As I entered my teenage years, the level of trouble escalated from neighborhood conflicts resolved by parents to run-ins with law enforcement settled in court. Throughout it all, my mother remained steadfast, always at the forefront, attempting to rescue me.

Even though I was often guilty of causing trouble, my mother remained convinced of my innocence. No amount of evidence or testimony could sway her belief. I never confessed to any wrongdoing either. Others would also make excuses for me, saying, "Alex is hanging out with the wrong crowd. Those guys are a bad influence on him." It wasn't until I reached adulthood that I came to the realization that the reason I was drawn to the wrong crowd was because I was part of it. I was just as much trouble as the others. That's why we clicked in the first place. Nobody forced me to follow along with the crowd. My grandmother had a saying, "Birds of a feather flock together."

My grandmother frequently became involved in my mother's and my own troubles, drawing us into her life. What grandmother wouldn't want to babysit her grandchild and offer assistance? However, few people were aware of my grandmother's struggles with violent mood swings. She could transition from being the sweetest grandmother to a brutal tyrant in a matter of minutes. Her insecurities often led her to express anger as a means of gaining a false sense of control over situations. Fear frequently gripped her. In today's context, she would likely have been diagnosed with schizophrenia and multiple personality disorder.

I have never forgotten the day she passed on to me the burden of anger she carried. I was a young kid playing in the yard with some cousins when suddenly she came bounding off the porch with fists balled and started punching me. She was a big woman, so it nearly knocked me off my feet. Still to this day, I have no idea why she pummeled me like that in front of all those kids. I remember my determination not to cry in front of everyone. I looked at her with a mix of emotions, but I said within myself, "No one will ever hurt me again." At that moment, I became a mini-version of her.

The same expression of anger she used would color my life for many years to come. Just like her insecurities prompted her to respond to life with anger, I found myself expressing anger to gain a sense of control over situations. I craved acceptance and respect among people. However, instead of fostering genuine connections, my anger led to superficial relationships governed by fear and tolerance. The anger that was lodged in my heart also fueled destructive behavior. The cartoon character, the Hulk, illustrates this reality.

Mild-mannered Bruce Banner had a monster inside him driven by rage. The anger within the character caused him to smash and destroy. Similarly, in my life, anger acted like a cancer that continued to grow. It shaded my outlook on life and jaded my personality. Eventually, it contributed to destroying relationships and fueled destructive impulses.

By the time I reached my late teens, I started hanging out with some African Americans in a rural Mississippi town. Back then, law enforcement didn't approve of whites and blacks socializing together. Being the only white guy in the group, I constantly felt the need to prove myself. The more reckless and audacious I acted, the more acceptance I garnered. I relished hearing them say, "That white boy is a fool!" At the time, there was no greater compliment in my eyes.

We were swiftly evolving into a gang. During this period, Hollywood was churning out movies centered around gangs, and the music industry was just starting to produce gangster rap. Truthfully, we aspired to emulate the individuals we admired in the media. One evening, we obtained firearms and made the decision to journey to a rival town to incite a confrontation. Unfortunately, during the altercation, a member of the rival group sustained a gunshot wound to the arm. Law enforcement promptly apprehended us and charged fifteen juveniles and two adults with the same violent offense.

I never saw my father throughout my entire life until the day I was arrested at seventeen years old, along with over a dozen other juveniles, for Aggravated Assault. When he arrived at the jail, he said, "I'm only here because it's mandated by law. Biologically, I'm your father, but I'll never be your daddy." I didn't know this man, so his words didn't have the sting he intended. I was looking at a stranger, but I always wondered what I could have possibly done to make him despise me like that.

The State of Mississippi determined that prosecuting me as an adult, assigning me a felony offense, removing me from my senior year of high school, and sending me to the Mississippi State Penitentiary among the most dangerous criminals in the state was in the best interest of all parties involved. In less than a year, I managed to return home due to good behavior. However, the toxic environment of prison left me psychologically scarred. Upon entering the system, I was desperate for a sense of self-worth, acceptance, significance, and purpose. Regrettably, the individuals I gravitated towards, who offered me these things, also introduced me to the opportunity to traffic drugs. Given my athleticism and muscular build, I found myself fitting well into the role of a collection agent. The more wild and reckless I behaved, the more respect and validation I received from my peers.

While based in Mississippi, the drug ring I was involved in expanded to include several stops in Louisiana. One night, on August 23, 1994, I woke from a nightmare with a distinct feeling that it wasn't an ordinary occurrence but rather a warning. In the dream, I saw a jail cell, and there was a suffocating sensation associated with it. Recognizing the gravity of the dream, later that day, I made the decision to leave Mississippi without informing my probation officer and headed to Lafayette, Louisiana, carrying a backpack filled with L.S.D. and Ecstasy. Around 1:00 A.M the following morning, I parked my brand-new Ninja Kawasaki motorcycle in my partner's front yard. He greeted me at the door, took possession of the drugs, and showed me to an extra bed. We began stirring around late that evening.

Two friends, deeply involved in drug trafficking, paid us a visit, prompting us to decide to head to a club. Around 9:30 P.M., all four of us crammed into one car and made our way to a dance club. Approximately two miles from my friend's house, a police car began tailing us. Later, authorities informed me that they had been surveilling my friend. Upon spotting my out-of-state license plate, they assumed I was the individual responsible for transporting drugs, prompting them to swiftly take action to apprehend us. Just as the officer activated his lights behind us, my friend who was driving handed me a cigarette pack containing ten tablets (commonly known as M.D.M.A. or XTC). He said, "Here Get rid of these!" Glancing behind me, I saw the police car right on our tail. Unable to dispose of the pills, I turned the box upside down and attempted to swallow its contents. Just two days prior to this incident, I had witnessed a girl overdose on two of those pills.

As we pulled over, I heard my friend shout, "The rest are in the glove compartment!" I quickly grabbed a plastic bag full of pills from the glove compartment and stuffed them down my pants. In less than thirty seconds, a policeman had me pressed against the hood of the car, along with the $6,097 cash I had in my pocket. The officers were on the lookout for drugs. The leading officer seemed convinced that they had caught us red-handed, but despite an extensive search, the team couldn't find anything. They even subjected my friends to strip searches on the side of the road. The frustration among the cops was palpable; they were certain they had us dead to rights.

At that point, I didn't know what had a hold on me! The drugs began to take effect. I felt like I was on another planet. Somehow, I managed to endure two hours' worth of interrogation on the side of the road.

Looking back, perhaps the cops were aware of my state. Maybe they were simply amusing themselves at my expense. However, after two hours, the officer in charge decided to try one last tactic to catch us. He said, "Okay, boys, here's the plan: we're going to put you guys in a car and take you back to where you came from. I'm going to search the house." (Even though they didn't have a search warrant.) "If we don't find anything, we'll let you go." The only problem with that plan was the backpack full of LSD on my friend's floor!

Suddenly, I found myself in a police car, being taken back to my friend's house. Ten minutes after arriving and searching the house, the head officer emerged and charged all four of us with possession of LSD with intent to distribute. Then, he confiscated my money and motorcycle. In exchange, I was given another felony charge: Money derived from drug proceeds. Just when I thought things couldn't get worse, the officer in charge remarked, "Well, look at that." Right across the street from my friend's house was an elementary school. Now, he was enhancing the offense to include that it was committed in a school zone.

Around midnight, we arrived at the Lafayette Parish Correctional Center. As we underwent the booking process, I requested permission from the officer to use the bathroom. With the realization that this might be my final visit, I entered the restroom. Retrieving the bag of pills concealed in my pants, I emptied a handful into my palm. In a drug induced haze, I murmured, "Goodbye, world," as I swallowed what I held and disposed of the remainder. Exiting the restroom, I tried to appear unaffected. The officer then escorted me to a holding cell, and upon looking up, fear engulfed me. It was the same jail cell I had seen in my nightmare nearly two days earlier. I staggered to the bed and collapsed.

As I lay there, the drugs exacted their punishment over the ensuing days. While I did not succumb to death, in the weeks that followed, I wished for it. The administration transferred me from the holding cell to the unit colloquially known as the "Crazy Pod," where individuals with mental health issues were housed. I contemplated ending my life by hanging, but lacked the strength to ascend high enough to tie the sheet. Depression enveloped me like a dark cloud, and I believed my life had reached its end. Not only did I face charges in Louisiana, but I also grappled with the realization that I had violated my probation in Mississippi by leaving the state without informing anyone.

My bond in Lafayette was set at $175,000. Before I could even consider the possibility of bonding out, Mississippi placed a detainer on me for a probation violation. It felt like a double blow. When Louisiana was done with me, Mississippi was coming for me too. I felt hopeless.

Then, one day, an inmate who was knowledgeable about Constitutional law came to clean up my housing unit. He inquired about my situation, and I disclosed everything to him. His response was surprising: "They can't do all that, man. That's illegal!" I stared at him in disbelief, but he assured me he was telling the truth. He suggested that I request permission to visit the law library and research the issue myself.

Upon investigating, I discovered that he was right about what he said. I promptly hired a lawyer who filed a motion to release me from the bond obligation. To my relief, the judge granted it. Freedom seemed within reach. Now, all I needed was to secure a lawyer in Mississippi and address the issue of leaving the state without permission. Legally, I had nothing against me except for that. Surely, they wouldn't want to impose a ten-year sentence just for failing to inform my probation officer before leaving the state.

Mississippi enacted the interstate compact agreement and extradited me back to Lamar County. Upon my return, I learned that my probation officer had resigned, and her husband, Mr. Bill Wallace, would be assuming her position. I retained a lawyer who engaged in discussions with Mr. Wallace regarding the possibility of reinstating my probation. Mr. Wallace conveyed that he was not opposed to the idea of giving me another chance and indicated that the ultimate decision rested with the judge, but he expressed a willingness to support the reinstatement of my probation.

Early one morning, Mr. Wallace presented me with a document to sign, without the presence of my lawyer. He assured me, "This is going to expedite things for you." Optimistically, I thought, "Great! I'll be home for Christmas." Hastily, I signed the paperwork and returned it to him. However, approximately two weeks later, I encountered Mr. Wallace in my vicinity and inquired about when I would be seeing the judge. To my shock, he chuckled and responded, "Son, don't you remember? You violated your probation two weeks ago. You're headed to the penitentiary." It dawned on me that he had deceived me into signing that document. Feeling betrayed, I immediately contacted my mother and uttered, "Mama, I won't be in jail for Christmas." True to my word, I escaped on the Thursday before Christmas and fled back to Louisiana.

I reached out to the drug dealers I was connected with and conveyed my urgency to leave the country. One night, I received a call from a dealer I knew from New York who was in Baton Rouge at the time. He asked me to handle some "dirty work" for him there. Needing the cash to facilitate my departure, I agreed to meet him. However, while carrying out the task, I was shot twice at point-blank range with a .357 Ruger loaded with hollow points.

My left lung was punctured, and my right leg was temporarily paralyzed. I lay on the ground that night, witnessing an animated blackness creeping towards me. As blood began to fill my chest cavity, the realization of imminent death struck me. It mirrored the suffocating feeling from a previous dream I had on August 23. Though lacking knowledge about God, I intuitively sensed I wasn't prepared to meet the Creator. In desperation, I cried out and begged for mercy.

The police and ambulance arrived simultaneously. An officer entered the back of the ambulance, leaning towards me and shouting, "You are dying! Tell me what happened before you die!" As my life slipped away, a sovereign decision by God intervened, halting death's grip on me.

I managed to reach the hospital in time, but the internal bleeding exerted pressure on my chest cavity, dangerously affecting my heart's function. The medical team opted to insert a chest tube through my rib cage to relieve the pressure and reinflate my collapsed lung. Thankfully, the procedure proved successful.

Two weeks later, as the nurses disconnected the final machine, a detective arrived to transport me to the East Baton Rouge Parish prison. There, I faced three felony charges and was classified as an escape risk, leading to my placement on Maximum Security lockdown.

My new abode was a cramped five by ten-foot cell, furnished only with a bed and a toilet, destined to be my sole companions for the next several months. Those initial months proved to be excruciating. I withdrew into myself, enveloped by a profound silence and an overwhelming desire to vanish from existence. I plummeted into the depths of the darkest depression I had ever known. Questions plagued my mind: Why was I even born? Why couldn't I simply fade into obscurity?

Security personnel regularly patrolled the premises, monitoring the inmates' activities. Usually, acquiring even an extra sheet of paper without the guards' knowledge proved futile. However, on this occasion, I managed to clandestinely obtain fifty Thorazine pills from a fellow inmate several cells above mine, evading the watchful eyes of security. In prison, where there's a will, there's always a way.

A war raged inside me. One part of me wanted to live, and another part of me wanted to die. I contemplated taking my life. The idea of ending it all seemed to offer a sense of control that was absent in my life. During those moments of planning my demise, I found temporary relief; however, a creeping fear would soon grip me at the notion of following through. What lies beyond? Is there a hell awaiting? Once you cross that line, there's no turning back. Would the God I called upon be disappointed that I didn't value the gift of another chance at life? Eventually, I reached a pivotal moment. I gathered my pills, stood up, gazed at them, and slowly watched each one tumble into the toilet. As the pills dissolved, I believed I had conquered my suicidal thoughts. I was mistaken.

Now, instead of simply hating life, I harbored a deep disdain for "everything living." My depression morphed into explosive anger, and my heart grew bitter. I shut out everyone, from guards to inmates to family members. I lashed out at the guards, testing if I could provoke them into ending my life. I actively sought out confrontations with anyone who crossed my path. I even resorted to throwing filthy toilet water at those who passed my cell. My appearance mirrored my tumultuous state – wild, disheveled hair and a long, unkempt beard. In the eyes of the staff, I was deemed mentally deranged, and I couldn't blame them. I had convinced myself that only a person plagued by madness would find themselves in such a dire situation.

One day, I found myself in a heated argument with another inmate who threw bleach on me. In my rage, I began howling and behaving erratically, almost like an animal. In response, the guards stripped me of all my belongings and shackled me naked to the cell bars. Fortunately, the head of Internal Affairs happened to be investigating a complaint nearby. Upon seeing my degrading state, he immediately rebuked the guards for their actions and ordered them to unshackle me.

Turning to me, he asked, "Son, are you crazy?"

"No," I replied, "but this environment is driving me to the edge. Imagine having a dog and keeping it confined without letting it out to run around. I need the chance to go outside."

According to the institution's regulations, they couldn't keep me locked up indefinitely without a proper hearing. Moreover, the security officers were clearly in the wrong for their treatment of me.

The Internal Affairs investigator presented me with an offer: if I maintained silence and exhibited good behavior for three weeks, he promised to facilitate my transfer to the general population. This reclassification would grant me access to outdoor activities three days a week. Although skeptical, I opted to play along with his proposition. Over the ensuing three weeks, I maintained a facade of sanity. As pledged, during the third week, the investigator coordinated with relevant authorities to release me from Maximum Security confinement. However, the outcome wasn't as expected; I found myself relocated to the prison's most notorious section. Barely five minutes beyond the Iron Gate, had I found myself embroiled in a brawl. The environment resembled a gathering of feral beasts, each vying for dominance.

Several months passed, and I found myself caught in a knife fight that resulted in a stab wound to my jaw. Fearing the repercussions of being labeled a confidential informant, I fabricated a story to security, claiming I had slipped in the shower. This falsehood was intended to prevent me from having to cooperate with security. Emergency medical staff transported me to the hospital for stitches. Upon my return to the prison, I was placed back in the same section where the altercation had taken place. A week later, around 9:00 P.M., I was once again stabbed, this time in my right eye. It wasn't until around 8:00 A.M. the following morning that I was finally seen by a doctor, who promptly performed surgery.

Following the surgery, the doctor informed me that my right tear duct had been irreparably damaged. As the swelling subsided, I regained partial vision in the eye. However, due to the destroyed tear duct, I had no control over my tears, which streamed down my face incessantly, resembling perpetual crying. My visage began to resemble a map of scars. The doctor explained that there was a corrective surgery available for my eye. This procedure involved drilling a hole in my nasal cavity, inserting a small tube through the hole, and positioning the other end beneath my eye. However, he cautioned that this surgery could potentially lead to further complications beyond my current issues. Ultimately, he recommended against pursuing it.

Upon my return to the prison, I was admitted to the infirmary. Meanwhile, my trial in Louisiana commenced. Just before proceedings were set to start, I discovered that my lawyer had declined a plea agreement with the District Attorney, all without informing me. Once I became aware of this, I expressed my desire to accept the plea deal. My lawyer assured me that he would work to reinstate the agreement. He, in turn, filed a motion to enforce the original plea agreement, arguing that his decision to reject it without affording me the opportunity to accept or reject it constituted ineffective assistance of counsel.

The District Attorney acknowledged that my lawyer had indeed done that, but she refused to reconsider the deal. With the judge prepared to proceed, he dismissed the motion. Trial proceedings commenced on Tuesday, and by Friday, the jury delivered the verdict: "We the people of the State of Louisiana find the defendant guilty!" As a result, I was promptly returned to prison.

In a brief span, I found myself in a confrontation within the infirmary with another inmate-patient. Consequently, I was relocated from the infirmary and returned to Maximum Security lockdown. The Internal Affairs investigator, who had assisted me previously, visited my cell and firmly stated that I would never leave lockdown again. He emphasized my perceived threat to the institution's security, other inmates, and even to myself. In his view, he was prepared to weld the door shut.

Chapter 2

New Birth

W

hile confined in my cell, I couldn't shake off the echo of the jury foreman's declaration: "Guilty!" The weight of having twelve individuals pronounce such a verdict and strip away everything dear to me felt unbearable. It led me to ponder what it would be like to stand before God and face His judgment. As I wrestled with these thoughts, a fellow inmate happened to pass by my cell, carrying a worn-out book destined for the trash. It was a battered copy of the Bible, its pages creased, and its paperback cover torn on one side. Intrigued, I called out to inquire about the book. He informed me it was a discarded Bible. Without hesitation, I requested it, feeling a compelling urge to explore the contents within its worn pages.

Instead of reaching for that proverbial shovel to dig myself back into a hole of depression, I opened the scriptures and began to read. Suddenly, the stories in the word of God came alive and had profound meaning. The crushing weight of guilt that I felt made sense—I was a sinner. My life had been lived in a materialistic, self-centered, rebellious way. However, if I would turn from my sinful life and way of thinking, and ask God to forgive me, He would. In fact, if I would place my faith in Jesus Christ and trust in His finished work at Calvary's cross, I would be saved from the judgment to come. While reading that Bible, I surrendered my heart to God and made Jesus the Lord of my life. Through that decision, I was born again, regenerated, and made a new creature in Christ (2 Cor. 5:17).

Discipline became a part of my life. Each morning, I woke up and prayed before starting the day, cultivating a relationship with my Savior. I spent most of my waking hours reading the scriptures. One day, I got the idea from the Bible to fast in order to draw closer to the Lord and gain a deeper understanding of what I was reading. Desiring education and growth in my spiritual walk, I asked the Lord for more understanding and even prayed for educational opportunities. To supplement my learning, I purchased a small, handheld radio with headphones to listen to local preachers on the airwaves. Additionally, a couple of inmates in neighboring cells possessed Christian books that they graciously allowed me to read. Through these avenues, God was healing my ravaged soul and discipling me in that lockdown cell.

The harsh, cold sting of the bars had vanished. For the first time, contentment permeated my being. Then one day, as I glanced at my reflection on the plastic cover of my radio, I noticed something peculiar: a smile adorning my face. A profound sense of peace and liberation washed over me, a sensation previously foreign in the world outside. Despite the presence of concrete, steel bars, and razor wire enclosing me, I felt liberated. Immersed in the scriptures, I savored moments of excitement and joy, finding the acceptance and significance my heart yearned for. Internally, transformations unfolded, novel experiences unfurling within me. And soon, physical changes would manifest as well.

The Holy Spirit used the passage from Isaiah 53:5 to begin the healing process and restore my eye. "He was wounded for our transgressions. He was bruised for our iniquities. The chastisement for our peace was upon Him, and *by His stripes we are healed.*" At that time, I didn't know about all the theological arguments against healing being a part of the believer's redemption in Christ, so they didn't get in the way. I innocently believed what I was reading. When I found the passage clarified in the New Testament in 1 Peter 2:24, the explanation settled the issue: "Who Himself bore our sins in His own body on the tree that we, having died to sin, could live unto righteousness *by whose stripes you were healed.*" I didn't have seven college degrees then, but I knew enough about English grammar that if my healing occurred nearly two thousand years ago at Calvary then it had to be available to me in the present. If I was healed (past tense), then obviously by faith I am healed (present tense).

Besides, following that reasoning is exactly how I was born again. I believed the first part of 1 Peter 2:24 that Jesus, the sinless Lamb of God, took my place on the cross. He took on the weight of sin and endured punishment on the cross on my behalf, granting me the precious gift of righteousness and the opportunity to live abundantly. Despite this pivotal event unfolding two millennia ago, my personal salvation didn't materialize until I embraced this profound truth. I also chose to believe in the second part of the scripture. Yet, as I gazed upon my reflection, I couldn't discern any immediate changes.

Tears continued to stream down my face, and the world around me seemed to echo the same old story of unchanging circumstances. Yet, I made a conscious decision to anchor my belief in the truth of God's word rather than the evidence of my surroundings. That night, as I lay down to rest, I lifted praises to God for what I had discovered in the scriptures, rather than dwelling on the reflection in the mirror.

Normally, upon waking, my right eye would be sealed shut by overnight drainage, necessitating a gentle massage with a damp cloth to open it. However, the following morning, both eyes opened effortlessly. At my subsequent doctor's appointment, he marveled, saying, "Son, it's incredible. Your eye is draining tears perfectly." Not only that, but during the vision test, I effortlessly read the eye chart with perfect 20/20 vision.

As I left the doctor's office that day, a glance in the mirror revealed that the scars on my face had miraculously faded. On the journey back to the prison, I made a solemn vow, saying, "Lord, wherever you lead me, whatever you ask of me, I'm yours." I wholeheartedly committed myself to serve the Lord faithfully in any circumstance that lay ahead.

God had plans to empower me to fulfill that prayer in ways that I did not expect. One evening, I borrowed a book on the Holy Spirit from another prisoner. After reading it, I realized that God the Father sent the Holy Spirit to fill and empower the believer for service. Once more, I wasn't aware of the theological arguments against receiving the Baptism in the Holy Spirit and speaking in other tongues, so they didn't hinder me. I was innocent and hungry for more of God. Once I realized that God had already sent the Spirit, just like salvation and healing, all I had to do was receive Him in greater measure. I raised my hands in that cell and began to speak in other tongues as the Spirit gave utterance.

Now, my Bible studies seemed even more intense. Each passage was speaking deeply and directly to me. I remember reading Matthew 28 concerning the Great Commission. Jesus came to his disciples and instructed them on their responsibility to the world as believers. He commanded them, "Go ye therefore, and teach all nations, baptizing them in the name of the Father, and the Son, and the Holy Ghost: Teaching them to observe all things whatsoever I have commanded you" (Mat. 28: 19, 20). As I was reading, I remember the Spirit of God whispering to my heart that He was going to use me in this manner. I quickly became excited at the idea, but then began to think, "How can you use me? I'm ignorant, uneducated, and I've made a mess out of my life?"

The Spirit of God impressed upon me the need to trust God and follow Him one day at a time. He assured me of His plan and promised to work everything out according to His purpose. I continued to immerse myself in the Word of God, allowing it to reshape my thinking. Through the Word, the Spirit of God was actively rewiring my cognitive processes. As I began to think differently in alignment with the Word, my behavior also began to reflect this transformation.

Something unexpected occurred in response to my prayer during the visit to the doctor's office. While I was studying in my cell, the electronic door suddenly slid open. I leaned out to see what the security officer needed. He instructed me to pack my belongings in a sheet; I was being relocated to the general population. A higher-ranking officer overheard and suspected a mistake. He attempted to halt the transfer, only to be informed that the order came from the top. His disbelief was palpable as he glanced at me. Privately, I thought, "Yes, it did indeed come from the highest authority." I bundled up my possessions in a sheet, slung them over my back, and proceeded towards my new housing assignment.

The new location had a very relaxed atmosphere. The unit housed approximately forty prisoners, comprising a mix of black, white, and Asian men. After spending a week there, I felt a prompting from the Lord to initiate a Bible study with the inmates. Within another week, twenty-four out of the thirty-nine men were attending regularly. During our sessions, we sang songs and I had the privilege of teaching a chapter of scripture, guided by the Lord. Following the teaching, we openly shared our problems and prayer requests.

During my time awaiting sentencing, I witnessed a steady stream of men coming and going. Some experienced a profound transformation, finding salvation through repentance and placing their faith in the Lord. Their lives were radically changed, with fractured family relationships being restored and young individuals being awakened from the brink of self-destruction. Addictions were overcome, illustrating the remarkable work of the Lord among these men who had been marginalized by society.

Since I wasn't from Baton Rouge, I didn't have any connections in the area. Once, during a period of lockdown, I made a statement expressing my reluctance to return to the place. Suddenly, I felt a strong impression from the Lord urging me to stay in Louisiana. Despite not knowing anyone in Baton Rouge who could offer me accommodation, and having depleted all my funds on legal expenses, I resolved to follow whatever path the Lord laid out for me.

A few days later, I received a letter from someone I hadn't seen in two years. The last time we had met, he was immersed in the same destructive lifestyle as I was. I had no idea what the content of the letter might be. It began, "Alex, one year and eight months ago, I surrendered my life to Christ. I've married my high school sweetheart, and I'm studying at a school just around the corner from you. God has called me into ministry. I care about you deeply, and I'd love to visit you. Please get in touch with me sometime." It was a surprise to reconnect with an old friend, especially one who had undergone such a transformative journey.

The Lord had orchestrated the arrival of a friend into my life, and I eagerly anticipated what the future held in store.

In the interim, I had the opportunity to encounter a guy who was relocated to my housing unit. He had previously witnessed my behavior in prison, where I had been far from exemplifying any sense of civility. However, upon seeing me this time, he was taken aback by the transformation. Gone was the chaos and danger he once associated with me. Instead, he saw a profound peace emanating from me, something undeniable. Intrigued, he couldn't resist approaching me and inquired, "What happened to you?" This question provided the perfect opening for me to share about my spiritual transformation and how the Lord had saved me. I took the opportunity to also impart the gospel to him. The encounter left a deep impression on him, prompting him to immediately call his parents and share the experience with them. Overwhelmed by the change they heard in their son's voice, they contacted their pastor, urging him to visit their son and learn more about his newfound faith.

Assistant Pastor Carl Everett from Bethany World Prayer Center graciously accepted the invitation to visit their son. During the visit, Pastor Carl provided counsel to the young man and offered to pray with him. Subsequently, the young man surrendered his heart to the Lord and committed to making Jesus the Lord of his life. Overwhelmed with emotion, he suggested that Pastor Carl also visit me. While I was engrossed in reading by my bed, I heard a guard call my name for a pastoral visit. Surprised, I queried the guard to ensure there wasn't a mistake regarding the visit. Reassured that it was indeed intended for me,

I welcomed the divine intervention that brought a pastor into my life, one who would continue to visit me in the weeks to come.

Over the ensuing months, my bond with Pastor Carl deepened until he felt like the father figure I had longed for. Our mutual affection was palpable; I cherished him, and he reciprocated that love. Together, our singular aim was to magnify and exalt Jesus Christ. One day, I confided in him my desire to refine myself for ministry and pursue higher education. A radiant smile adorned his face as he responded, "I'd be honored to recommend you for admission to the Minister Training Institute (M.T.I.)." Bethany World Prayer Center hosted a school dedicated to nurturing leaders for ministry, but each applicant required an endorsement from a Christian leader to gain entry. It felt as though my newfound aspiration was falling into place. I envisioned remaining in Louisiana, attending school for ministry, all in the pursuit of better serving the Lord.

A few days later, my lawyer paid me a visit with surprising news. He relayed that the District Attorney lacked the necessary paperwork to pursue an enhanced sentence against me, potentially leading to a more lenient sentence with credit for time already served. Remarkably, Mississippi had agreed to relinquish jurisdiction over my case to Louisiana. They no longer sought to extradite me to face the consequences of my actions. Consequently, upon the judge's pronouncement of "Credit for time served," I would be free to go. But to where? I found myself in need of a place to stay while reintegrating into society. The thought crossed my mind to approach my friend who was attending school, but I hesitated. He had recently married and was navigating his own academic pursuits. Moreover, being new to the area, I couldn't bear the thought of disrupting his newly established life.

Nevertheless, the Lord impressed upon me to ask him. I decided to swallow my pride and ask him the next visiting day. Visiting day came around, and so did my friend. During our visit, I kept putting off asking him if I could temporarily stay with him. Towards the end of our time together, my friend said, "I want to ask you a favor." "Anything," I said. "You name it." He replied, "I want you to pray about something. My wife and I want you to come and stay with us when you get out." I was speechless. I finally told him, "I wanted to ask you, but I was concerned it was too much to ask." He said he was afraid that I was going to turn him down, so he'd been putting it off. The plan seemed to be coming together. I had a place to stay. I had my pastor recommending me for school. Two days later, I would be going to court and expecting to walk out the gates to my new future.

The big day arrived. I woke up that morning with a sense of peace and joy in my heart. Throughout the morning and all the way to the courthouse, I prayed in the Spirit. Even in the courtroom, the Holy Ghost was bubbling out of me. He kept whispering scriptures to comfort me. When my turn came around, and I stood before the judge, he spoke: "In view of this matter, Mr. Hennis, I'm going to give you forty years, day for day, no probation, no parole." His words far exceeded the sentencing guidelines which didn't carry a fraction of that time. The District Attorney never produced the necessary paperwork for the judge to enhance my sentence. Despite hearing the judge's words, the joy of the

Lord never left my heart. Once again, the Holy Ghost whispered, "Trust in the Lord with all your heart and lean not unto your own understanding" (Proverbs 3:5). "I will never leave you or forsake you" (Hebrews 13:5).

I walked out of that courtroom with the creator of the universe inside me. John wrote, "Greater is he that in you than he that is in the world" (1 John 4:4). As the guards transported me back to the prison, I prayed, "Lord, wherever you want me to go, I will go; whatever you want me to do, I will do it." He was sustaining me through this unexpected event. I wanted to serve him. I was convinced that God was not through with me yet. The scripture came to mind, "Though he slay me, yet will I trust him" (Job 13:15). Walking through the lower part of the courthouse, the guards had to place me in a cell while one officer retrieved the car. A prostitute and a woman facing drunk driving charges were in the cell next to me. Curiosity got the best of them; they asked me for my story. I was happy to tell them.

I witnessed to both ladies about God's saving grace. The poor prostitute didn't believe she was worth saving. I encouraged her to open her heart to Jesus, assuring her that he wouldn't take advantage of her. The alcoholic lady listened intently. They were awestruck by my peace despite receiving such bad news. Before the guards arrived to take me away, I asked if I could pray for them, and they both agreed. No sooner had I finished my prayer than the guards were there to escort me. Upon returning to the prison, the men who knew of my situation patiently awaited the outcome of my sentencing. Many had been praying for me. A crowd greeted me as I entered the housing unit. I informed them of my sentence. Some thought I was joking, some shook their heads in disbelief, and some even became angry. Nevertheless, I resumed where I left off and led the day's Bible study.

I remained there for several weeks, ministering and touching lives. Then, one night, security woke me up and ordered me to pack all my belongings. I was being transferred from the Parish prison to Elayn Hunt Correctional Center for processing into the Louisiana Department of Corrections and subsequent transfer to another facility. Upon arrival at Hunt, all my belongings were confiscated. I was stripped of my clothing, given a jumpsuit, and placed in a lockdown cell with another individual. This young man had been subjected to a harrowing experience—he had been raped and coerced into prostitution while housed in another Parish prison. Eventually, I managed to persuade a guard to procure a Bible from the chaplain's department. I began reading it aloud with the young man in the cell.

One evening, an officer made his way down the line of cells, informing each inmate of their transfer to another facility. When he reached our cell, he lowered his head and whispered, "You two are being transferred to Angola. God help you." I couldn't grasp why he was adding such drama to our transfer to Angola, but the young man beside me understood all too well. He spiraled into hysteria. The dread of reliving his experiences at the parish prison now awaited him as his daily reality in Angola until his last breath. With a life sentence without parole, his fate seemed sealed.

My perspective differed. I felt a divine calling to these men. They weren't just prisoners; they were individuals cherished by God, and I believed He intended to use me as a vessel to reach them. In my eyes, Angola wasn't just a prison—it was my mission field. Regardless of what lay ahead, my sole desire was to remain faithful to the Lord.

Chapter 3

The Farm

W

hen I arrived at Angola, it was winter. The officer in charge of processing new arrivals into the prison decided to welcome us by leaving us outside in the cold with short sleeves and no shoes. Once the classification department looked at my records, they placed me in the Working Cell blocks. There, men were housed in two-man cells, but during the day, we worked the cotton and vegetable fields. Each workday, we were issued tools and marched at gunpoint to certain sections of the prison to work the land and cultivate the crops. Often, prisoners used those tools to maim and kill each other. The work was arduous, and the conditions, bitter cold in the winter and scorching heat during the summer, were punishing. Officers stood by with automatic weapons to stop fights and prevent escapes. They offered one warning shot for inmates to voluntarily stop fighting or fleeing; the next bullet was meant to kill. One way or another, the fight or the escape stopped. In the end, the administration was in control.

I never saw my previous cell mate again once we were shipped to Angola. Men who were in his position only had three options: a life of slavery by belonging to another inmate, escape, or suicide. I ended up with a new cell mate in the working cell blocks who was doing time for Armed Robbery. He decided he didn't want to work in the grueling field conditions anymore. He was going to force the administration to place him on lockdown. When it was time to go to work, he stayed in the cell. Soon, an officer came to escort him to administrative lockdown until he went to disciplinary court. When he went before the disciplinary board, the chairman told him that he wasn't going to place him on lockdown for not going to work. He informed him that he would have to hurt someone for him to do that. My cellmate, in turn, told the chairman that he would take care of that part. Considering I was in the cell with him, I made the most reasonable target.

Thick fog had descended on the prison grounds that morning. The entire facility was on lockdown until it lifted, ensuring no one could exploit the fog as cover for escape. From my perch on the top bunk, I overheard the exchange between my cell mate and the chairman at the top of the tier of cells. I even caught sight of the knife as an inmate passed it to him through the bars. Honestly, I didn't harbor any desire to attack this man. I had poured out my heart to him, witnessing about God's saving grace. Rolling over, I resigned myself to the Lord, expressing readiness to go if He called. Suddenly, all the cell doors swung open. The officer in charge bellowed, "Work call!" The fog had dissipated, and it was time for everyone to report for duty. Donning my boots, I joined the stream of inmates heading out the gate. As we reached the field, the sound of a scuffle erupted to my left.

My cellmate opted to head to work, leaving his knife concealed in the cell. As we marched into the field, he engaged in a heated exchange with another inmate, who then attacked him with a large gardening hoe. When the assailant lost his weapon, my cellmate resorted to an unexpected tactic, sinking his teeth into the attacker's neck. Given his broken and jagged teeth, this unconventional defense proved remarkably effective, resembling something out of a zombie scenario.

Suddenly, a gunshot shattered the tense atmosphere. Everyone dropped their tools and retreated from the scene. Trucks promptly arrived, and prison officials swiftly restrained the two fighting inmates, binding them like wild game trophies before hauling them away in the back of a truck.

Upon returning to the cell blocks, I learned that an Administrative Board would convene soon to assess eligibility for transfer to the general population.

During my time working in the field, I often found myself navigating a perilous balance between violent inmates and abusive officers. Some inmates resorted to attacking others simply to prompt a transfer to another section of the prison—a tactic commonly known as "using someone up." Meanwhile, certain problematic officers engaged in a disturbing competition, betting on who could write up and discipline the most inmates, regardless of their guilt or innocence. Amidst these challenges, I endeavored to keep a low profile, working diligently while avoiding unnecessary attention.

Each day presented an opportunity for me to share my faith with those around me. Amidst the exertion of physical labor and the heaviness of the environment, I would share my testimony and speak of God's saving grace. One particular day, an abusive officer, typically seen atop a horse and armed, unexpectedly summoned me to speak with him. Setting aside his usual demeanor, he handed his weapon to another officer and approached me with a sense of vulnerability. He confessed his intention to harass me, yet something restrained him. Clearly shaken, he admitted, "I usually do as I please, to whomever I choose. But I can't explain what stopped me. Who are you?"

This encounter provided a profound opportunity for me to share the transformative message of Jesus Christ with him.

A couple of days after my cellmate's altercation, I was assigned a new one. He was a drug dealer convicted of murder and kidnapping. While in Parish prison awaiting trial for these offenses, he was caught attempting to have a firearm smuggled into the facility. He confided in me about a plan he and his associates had devised. They intended to use the weapon to stage a non-lethal shooting among themselves and then frame an Asian inmate for the incident. Their scheme aimed to portray the Asian inmate as the aggressor who had shot them before turning the gun on himself. By fabricating this scenario, they hoped to leverage potential lawsuits to mitigate their criminal charges.

I eventually shared my story and asked him if he would be willing to make Jesus the Lord of his life. He mocked my faith and said Christianity was a tool to control black people. He claimed that he was a Muslim. He also suggested that as a white man, I was using religion because I feared prison life. I never argued with him over his false accusations. Instead, I continued to show kindness toward him and demonstrate my faith. One day, he told me that I should go to the Main prison and join the Bible College. I thought to myself, "Is there really a Bible College here?" I had no idea if it was true.

The Administrative Board finally arrived to determine who was eligible to transfer to the general population. When I had the chance to address the board, I expressed my desire to attend church and experience some of the benefits of being in the general population. After reviewing my records, the Major in charge stated, "I'm going to send you to the Main prison. Son, if you can't survive, let one of us know. We'll get you out of there." At the time, I was so new to the culture that I didn't realize he was attempting to disrespect me. Instead, I interpreted his words as genuine concern for my wellbeing. It wasn't until later that I understood he was actually suggesting that I wasn't able to take care of myself, which was considered an ultimate putdown in Angola. At that moment, I had no clue.

The Main prison is where the majority of Angola's inmates are housed. This section of Angola was designed in the 1950s with dormitories and an Education building. Inmates are permitted to attend classes and participate in club activities such as Toastmasters, Dale Carnegie, and Alcoholics Anonymous. They elect representatives and adhere to standardized curriculums. Of particular significance to me, inmate pastors regularly conducted church services, a practice uncommon in most prisons across America. Here is some of the history that elucidates how Angola developed this model.

Robert F. Kennon became governor of Louisiana in 1952 and sought to fulfill his campaign promise to reform Angola following a severe scandal that transpired under Governor Earl K. Long's administration. Thirty-one white prisoners resorted to slashing their Achilles tendons with a razor blade rather than venturing into the cane fields, citing overwork, brutality, abysmal living conditions, and extreme physical punishment. Governor Kennon promptly directed the Hospital Board, responsible for the prison, to engage a competent professional penologist to oversee its management. They were afforded the rare opportunity to select a qualified individual for the role, as no political commitments had been made regarding Angola. This marked a notable departure from the circumstances preceding the scandal.

Governor Kennon requested an initial $4 million from the Legislature to commence the construction of an enhanced facility, with an additional $4 million earmarked for subsequent phases. Thus, construction of the Main prison complex, prioritizing education and rehabilitation, was completed in 1955. Funds were also allocated to enhance compensation for civilian guards and bolster officer recruitment. To economize years prior, the state had armed inmates with shotguns to oversee fellow inmates.

The Governor's initial plan aimed to reduce the number of convict guards, who were seen as a necessary evil. However, this plan never materialized. Consequently, Louisiana resorted to using armed inmates to guard their fellow inmates until the 1970s. The horrors resulting from this methodology would require an entire book to fully capture. In the meantime, Reed Cozart, an outsider who served as the director of the federal penitentiary in Texas, worked tirelessly to usher in reform and dismantle the ruthless regime that controlled Angola Penitentiary. However, both he and the Governor faced resentment and resistance from the southern Democrats who remained in power, viewing them as unwelcome northern outsiders.

Maurice Sigler, who officially assumed the role of warden in December 1952, was a seasoned penal professional with ties to Cozart. He enjoyed the full support of Governor Kennon. Warden Sigler was acutely aware of the challenges he faced upon taking office. In a 2000 interview with The Angolite, he reflected, "I was not welcome here. This was a time of deep segregation. You simply didn't advocate for black people. But I held firm to my own beliefs and upbringing, believing in these rehabilitative programs." Unfortunately, his vision never materialized due to political obstacles and a lack of funding. Nonetheless, he permitted the establishment of inmate-led churches and organizations, although he lacked the resources to hire professional staff and disarm the inmate guards.

Before Governor Kennon's building projects of the 1950s were completed, the prison housed two similar church buildings situated opposite each other in the middle of the prison grounds: one for Protestant services and the other for Catholic services. Each weekend, two services were held in each chapel. The first service catered to the employees, or "free people," while the second was for the inmates.

Since 1908, a contract chaplain had served both the Protestant and Catholic faiths, although their involvement in the inmates' spiritual well-being was minimal, often limited to delivering death messages related to an inmate's family.

Inmate Clifford Hampton arrived at Angola in 1964, nearly twelve years after Governor Kennon's building projects and efforts to reform Angola had commenced. However, the inmates showed little interest in attending church. Hampton remarked, "They were interested in staying alive." According to him, church services were primarily attended by individuals seeking sexual encounters, particularly with homosexuals. Occasionally, a prisoner's homosexual partner might be housed in another section of the prison, prompting the church to serve as a rendezvous point for them. The prevalence of such perversions was so widespread that Hampton likened the situation to the conditions of the temple during the reign of King Manasseh (2 Kings 21).

Once the Main prison was operational, inmates were allowed to gather unsupervised in rooms upstairs in the Main prison's education building to hold church services, but they didn't carry Bibles with them. Instead, they carried knives. The prevailing sentiment was, "It's better to be caught by security with a knife than to be without it in the presence of another prisoner." These rooms served as a central meeting ground where inmates could acquire illegal drugs, homemade wine known as "hooch," or even engage male prostitutes. One prisoner remarked that during the sixties and seventies, some inmate preachers possessed more homosexual slaves than anyone else. To gain any semblance of authority or respect in Angola, one had to cultivate an aura of danger and fear. Much like the jungle, the strong preyed upon the weak.

During the 1970s and 1980s, federal intervention occurred in the penitentiary due to a lawsuit alleging "cruel and unusual punishment." Angola had long held a reputation as one of the most notorious prisons, encompassing the bloodiest 18,000 acres in America. Another reform-minded warden, Ross Maggio, assumed leadership to quell the violence and establish order throughout the prison. As he gained control over prison-wide violence, efforts toward spiritual and moral reform seeped into the church. External volunteers commenced working with the inmate-led churches, introducing Bible teaching and education into the prison system. Although gradual, the wheels of change began to set in motion.

Upon my arrival into the system, there were five official inmate-led churches recognized at the Main prison, alongside one Jehovah's Witness congregation and one Islamic service. However, only seven hundred prisoners out of five thousand were attending a service at least once a month. Around this same time, a charismatic renewal swept through all five Protestant churches. The church leadership and significant portions of the congregations underwent baptism in the Holy Spirit, evidenced by speaking in tongues (Acts 2:4). This experience served as a catalyst for more intense growth, development, and discipleship across the inmate-led churches.

During this period, Warden Burl Cain assumed control of the prison. Recognizing the potential of the church as a solution to Angola's problems, he chose to collaborate with the ongoing changes. He extended an invitation to the New Orleans Baptist Theological Seminary to establish a regionally accredited college program within the heart of the Main prison, aimed at better training church leaders.

Within this context, I arrived at the Main Prison. I was reclassified to the West Yard and placed in the field. This assignment begins a person at the bottom of the general population hierarchy. The grueling work was similar to that of the Working Cell Blocks, but I had the privilege of living in a dormitory and spending time outdoors. Additionally, I was able to participate in approved social activities and attend church. Many inmates were discussing transitioning from field work to securing a job within the Main Prison's compound, with the eventual goal of obtaining trustee status. I discovered that there were numerous benefits associated with having a job. Furthermore, employment offered the opportunity to relocate to the East Yard, which experienced far less violence and chaos compared to the West Yard. Prisoners were more settled, and the guards were less oppressive. Essentially, these inmates worked diligently to avoid trouble and enjoy the advantages of residing on the "job side."

For some reason, no one in classification responded to my request for a job. I continued to toil in the field with no end in sight. The field work was brutal, reminiscent of the Israelites laboring under Pharaoh's rule. After several months passed, I received a rejection notice in the prison mail regarding my job request. The denial stated that it was at the board's discretion to decline my application, suggesting that I should reapply in six months' time. Taking the denial to the Lord in prayer, I found solace. While it seemed impossible in the natural to secure a job once rejected by the board, I clung to the belief that with God, all things are possible. I dared to have faith that God would pave a way in this seemingly impassable situation.

A couple of days later, while we were waiting to pass through the gate to begin our field work, an officer approached me and asked for my name. He then instructed me and several others to report to the captain's office. While most of the guys walking back with me anticipated trouble, my mindset had shifted. I no longer viewed situations in that light. Instead, I held onto the belief that God was in control and had my best interests at heart when guiding the course of my life. Ultimately, I was convinced that whatever lay ahead was something good.

As it turned out, this group had been selected for a special assignment by the overseer of our field work. Due to my diligent work ethic and absence of complaints, I had earned a spot on his list. My prayers had been answered. While I would still be residing in the West

Yard, they moved me to another section and dormitory within it. Monday through Friday, I spent my time sorting vegetables at the Grading Shed and tried to connect with the men around me. Each day brought uncertainty; the sporadic outbreaks of violence had a way of disrupting our routines. Strangely enough, it seemed that one of my previous job requests had crossed a Classification officer's desk. After a few months at the Grading Shed, I was offered a position at the prison's Print Shop. This new job necessitated an immediate transfer to the East Yard.

Chapter 4

The Transition Begins

D uring this time, I also became involved with the inmate churches. Previously, I had never stood behind a pulpit and preached, but an inmate pastor singled me out from the crowd and said, "Share what God's put on your heart." He handed over the service to me. Filled with the word and love for the Lord, I preached as if it were second nature. When I finished, the room erupted into spontaneous singing. Later, I met some prisoners who were attending Bible College. They were deeply moved by the service and suggested that I enroll in the school. I didn't need an angel appearing to me or a burning bush experience to make my decision. I could either continue working at a prison job or devote myself to studying the word of God full-time. I obtained an enrollment form and signed my name on it. In my naivety, I didn't anticipate that this action would upset my job supervisor.

I often witnessed a state employee stealing thousands of dollars' worth of material from various job sites on the Main prison compound. Despite this, I chose to remain silent. I worked diligently and kept my mouth shut. When I informed him of my decision to transfer to Bible College, he grew enraged and threatened that the only way I would leave the job was if he confined me to solitary. Oddly, despite my hard work, silence, and lack of complaints, he had no intention of letting me go. Instead, he made daily threats that he would falsely write me up and ruin my chances for good if I attempted to transfer. It was crucial for an inmate to maintain a relatively good disciplinary record to enroll in school. Fortunately, God's plan for my life prevailed over any schemes my supervisor might have had to keep me there.

Within a few weeks of enrolling in school, I returned to the dorm after work and received a notice from an officer instructing me to report to the Bible College for my new job assignment. I was now officially a student of New Orleans Baptist Theological Seminary. No longer was I required to report to the print shop. As part of the enrollment process, I also needed an inmate pastor to sign a recommendation for me to enroll. He had to confirm on record that he recognized the calling on my life and attest that I faithfully attended his fellowship. I obtained this recommendation without any issues.

When I arrived at the Main prison, I had joined one of the churches, and a few weeks later, I was elected by the members to a position on the leadership board. Because I was a new member, I wasn't aware of the internal politics happening behind the scenes. A large part of the congregation was trying to elect me to the position of Assistant Pastor because they appreciated the way God was using me in the prison. They were also upset with the lack of zeal in the present Assistant Pastor. I didn't know the head pastor was also fearful of losing his position. Suddenly, I was involved in a conflict and didn't even know it. After the election, the pastor approached me and told me that he didn't want me on his board. However, he signed my recommendation to enroll in Bible College, but I was never allowed to preach in his service again. After one year of inactivity, I left the service.

One night, I stumbled upon a Spirit-filled chaplain, Gregory Green, who was hosting a meeting. Gregory Green had been a professional basketball player, but God called him out of his sports career and into ministry. After training at a Charismatic Bible College, he applied for an assistant chaplain position at Angola. In fact, he experienced an open vision of the Lord in a prison cell that confirmed his calling to preach in prison. During his services, the gifts of the Spirit manifested, and some of the most depraved prisoners were gloriously saved and delivered from demonic bondage. Often, he would step down from the pulpit and point to someone, telling them the Lord said for them to preach. These were equally explosive times. The Spirit continued to manifest in supernatural ways, and men were set free.

Once, Chaplain Green felt led by the Lord for us to hold hands and form a circle in the chapel. As forty-five prisoners sang, the power of the Lord fell and knocked everyone to the floor. This experience reminded me of when the priests could not stand in the temple because of the presence of the Lord (2 Chron. 5:14). The security officer observing the service got so scared, he hit the emergency button on his radio and summoned extra security to the scene. The officer couldn't understand or explain the situation, so the administration put the service under investigation.

During another service, I was instructed to share what the Lord had placed on my heart. After preaching and leading several men to the Lord, the congregation burst into song. No one wanted to leave the service because of the Lord's presence. When the security personnel came and told us that we had to disperse, everyone marched together through the prison, singing over and over, "Holy, Holy, Holy is the Lord!" This unusual activity caused the inmate population to wonder what was causing the commotion, so they started attending the following services to see for themselves.

The Lord often worked through the chaplain to call men forward and reveal details about their personal lives. For instance, two men he called forward were discussing a drug deal outside the chapel where no one could hear; however, the Spirit heard and relayed the information to the chaplain. He, in turn, called them forward and recounted exactly what they had said and planned. They admitted their sin and asked for forgiveness.

When the Lord would use a leader to single me out to preach, I would follow the Spirit's leading and witness some of the hardest prisoners being set free. We often witnessed manifestations of demons that had plagued these men's lives. At the name of Jesus, those spirits relinquished their control over them and departed. In this setting, I learned to follow the Spirit's leading, minister, and preach.

For a period, the established inmate pastors were attending to hear the chaplain flow in the prophetic ministry. Congregants from each inmate-led church were also present. The body of Christ in Angola seemed to be uniting under a central head until the chaplain began calling the pastors to accountability and holiness. Some of these men were walking closely with the Lord, while others were involved in gross immorality. Until then, the inmate leaders had lacked accountability.

These men were elected to their positions, and the only way they could be removed was through an election held every two years. When the Spirit continued to press for repentance, some of the pastors who were persisting in sin ceased attending the services. However, their departure didn't occur until after a warning had been issued.

One night, the chapel was packed, and we were worshiping with great intensity. The Spirit began to speak through the minister and warn those who held positions of authority in the church. If the pastors did not heed the call to repent and realign their lifestyle with God's word, their lives were at stake. In other words, these men would face death if they didn't reconcile with God.

Over the next several years, I witnessed the diagnosis of terminal diseases or the succumbing to heart failure of half of those leaders. Over time, others who had refused to repent were publicly exposed for their unrepentant sins and consequently removed from ministry. These men were resistant to the change that the Lord desired to bring inside the prison, clinging onto power instead of surrendering control to the Lord. Meanwhile, I regularly convened with several men from each congregation once a week in the Education building. Together, we fervently prayed for revival and the transformation of the prison. Reflecting on those times, I am convinced that much of the radical change that occurred in Angola over twenty-five years was birthed in that prayer room. For at least three hours a week, we wept for the souls of men to be saved and prayed for church authorities. Additionally, we committed to fasting and praying for the Lord to develop the churches and use us as agents of change. This intercession persisted for several years.

Around this time, Warden Cain made the decision to rebuild Angola's renowned Prison Rodeo Arena, making it bigger and better, with a seating capacity of 10,500 people. Once a year, every Sunday in October, and later one weekend in April, prisoners from the general population could sign up and participate in an actual rodeo, regardless of their experience level. Tickets were sold to the public, drawing attendees from around the world to witness what was billed as "The Wildest Show in the South."

During the construction of the new arena, I perceived with spiritual insight and prophesied during our prayer group that the arena would be utilized to glorify God. It would become a venue for the preaching of the gospel, attracting people from all corners of the globe to be a part of the Angola revival.

Over time, that's precisely what transpired. Christian influencers from across the country began holding services in the rodeo arena, drawing in worshiping inmates who consistently filled the stands. On several occasions, when renowned Christian leaders such as Billy Graham held services, the prison administration permitted the public to attend alongside the inmates. Daily, cultural shifts were occurring within the prison walls.

As word of the revival continued to spread across the nation, Wheaton Bible College took a keen interest in the movement. Many of their alumni were actively involved in the spiritual outpouring within the prison. Deeply moved by the evident work of the Spirit, college officials regularly arranged for their students to visit Angola during Spring break. These young men and women were welcomed into the prison community, socializing with us and attending our church services.

After spending a day fellowshipping with the Christian community, these young visitors expressed feeling a profound sense of safety. One young man candidly confessed, "I don't understand it. You guys don't have anything, but you are so happy. We have so much, but we don't have the joy that you have." These encounters left a lasting impact on the visitors, as they departed Angola with a renewed perspective on life and faith.

My experience with the rodeo arena was about to take on another dimension. A few months before I enrolled in Bible College, a prisoner named Bullfighter, whom I was actively sharing my faith with, asked if I was interested in participating in the rodeo. Registration forms were being circulated in each housing unit for those interested in signing up. As long as I didn't have any medical conditions that prevented participation, all I had to do was indicate the events I wanted to participate in, sign my name, and submit the form to the captain's office. On the day of the rodeo, a list of participants was circulated throughout the prison to organize our travel to the arena.

You have to understand, the closest thing to a bull that I'd ever been near was a quarter pounder at McDonald's. Nevertheless, filled with faith and the belief that "I could do all things through Christ," I eagerly accepted the challenge. In my naivety, I assumed that included rodeo.

When Bullfighter asked if I was interested, I replied without hesitation, "Sure, I'll do it." Checking off every event listed on the registration sheet, I committed fully. A couple of weeks later, as the rodeo commenced and I sat among the participants with thousands of eyes on us, an inmate was injured, and an opportunity for a bull ride unexpectedly arose. The officer in charge urgently called out, "I need a bull rider!"

Reacting without a second thought, I raised my hand and volunteered, "I'll do it." The officer, clearly surprised, questioned me, "Alex, have you ever ridden a bull before?" Being a Christian, I couldn't bring myself to lie.

I told him that I had ridden a jackass and a milk cow at a friend's house once. Unfortunately, he misunderstood me, thinking I was being facetious. He exclaimed, "All right! We got a cowboy, folks. Put him on." In just a few short minutes, I found myself straddling a bull with my hand tied in a rope.

As the guys above me asked if I was ready, I mustered a shaky, "Yeah." Suddenly, someone outside snatched the gate open, and that's the last thing I recall. The next moment, I found myself standing up, knocking the dust off me. To my amazement, people started pouring out of the stands, congratulating me with pats on the back, exclaiming, "Way to ride, cowboy!"

Feeling both surprised and amused by the unexpected turn of events, I decided the only fitting thing to do was to purchase a black Stetson cowboy hat and embrace my newfound role as the Christian cowboy.

Although I didn't know anything about rodeo, the Lord granted me success and favor in the sport for years to come. My life and ministry within the prison took on a new dimension. Suddenly, television cameras, newspapers, and magazines were eager to speak with me. It wasn't unusual to have a film crew follow me around the prison to create a documentary. Journalists were always surprised that instead of a hardened convict cowboy, I was a humble Christian. They were interested in hearing rough stories about prison life, but I focused on the revival occurring in Angola. I emphasized how Jesus changed my life, and how the same gospel message had brought blacks and whites together to create a better world inside the penitentiary. Honestly, they were blown away.

My success in the rodeo and Christian confession didn't always sit well with everyone. After a successful ride, I bowed my knee in the arena and pointed to heaven. Later, security officers would hurl terrible insults to my face and even express wishes for my demise. When I conducted interviews with everyone from CNN to NBC to the Boston Globe, some prison officials and security officers were offended. These men and women were angered by the fact that the Warden was elevating us to star status. While these interviews were Warden Cain's idea, they hesitated to express their feelings to him out of fear. Nevertheless, their fear of Cain didn't deter them from attempting to make my life miserable. Despite winning nearly every event and the championship buckle that accompanied them, I was driven by a particular desire to win one specific buckle: the All-Around championship.

I trained hard physically and overcame injuries. I racked up multiple concussions: a fractured skull, a fractured scapula, broken legs, broken ribs, a punctured lung, cracked vertebrae, and torn ligaments, just to name a few. (Yes, the list is longer. USA Today did an article on us that included about half my injuries.) Nonetheless, I pursued the championship with abandon. This determination made my enemies even angrier. Finally, I won the buckle I wanted. The London Times was there to interview me as the winner. This publication took my Christian testimony back to England and around the world. Sadly, several months later, when we had the awards ceremony in the prison, the officials who were against me gave my buckle to someone else. With one administrative decision, they robbed me of something I had striven so hard to achieve. Instead of getting mad and walking away, I determined that I would try even harder again.

During one attempt to win the buckle, I broke my lower leg in the rodeo. A bareback horse ran my leg down the chute and twisted my foot backward. The doctor was contemplating putting screws in my fibula. I asked for a medical refusal form to sign. I told them that I didn't want medical attention at that time. If you were treated at the hospital and given a "duty status" which relieved you from work, you could not participate in the rodeo. Since there was only one rodeo left and I was in the lead, I decided to deny medical attention and wait until after the last rodeo to deal with my leg. I needed one successful bull ride to win the All-Around buckle. I signed the necessary paperwork to discharge me and limped back to the housing unit.

In a short time, the administration and inmate population knew about my situation and injury. A lot of the guys started pulling for me to win. One guy who was known for getting whatever a person wanted in the prison decided to do me a favor. This inmate showed up in front of my bed with a set of crutches. Normally, security officers would take something like this from you if the medical staff had not assigned them to you, but the kinder officers knew I needed some help. Everyone played dumb.

I made it through the week without any questions from security, but my leg and ankle were swollen. On the day of the last rodeo, the guys in my dorm formed a line from the microwave to the bathroom. One guy heated a container of water in the microwave and passed it to the next guy, and so on. Meanwhile, I placed my foot and leg in a mop bucket, and as the water was passed down the line, it was poured into the bucket. This process was repeated with several containers multiple times until the bucket was full. They were helping me reduce the swelling so I could get my boot over my foot and ankle. Eventually, we succeeded in getting it over my foot, and I laid my crutches down and hobbled to the rodeo arena.

That day, I participated in several events before my bull ride. I got hammered multiple times in those events, and everyone thought it was the end of me. Somehow, I managed to get up each time and continue participating. Despite the challenges, I maintained my lead in the points, but I needed a successful bull ride to clinch the All-Around buckle. Luckily, I drew a good bull and had a fair chance of staying tied to him in the chute. When I nodded my head, the ground men jerked the chute door open.

He exploded instantly outside the gate. During those moments, its odd how long eight seconds feel, and how much thought goes through your mind in that short time period. Towards the end of the ride, I felt my hand slipping out of the rope and my leg began to give way. In a flash, I found myself on the ground. Just then, I heard the buzzer. I missed it by a fraction of a second.

The emptiness and despair that hit you in that moment is awful, but I couldn't survive in prison wallowing in self-pity. In those moments, I had to get up, shake the dust off, give thanks to God, and get the job done next time. That's my basic philosophy when it comes to dealing with life's difficulties. Ironically, none of my competitors rode a bull successfully that day either. I was clearly the point's leader. However, the administrative officials who had taken my previous buckle away decided that no one would be awarded this buckle. For the first time in the history of the rodeo, no All-Around buckle would be awarded. This time, they would not refer to the point's leader.

I didn't have time to feel sorry for myself. I had to get to the hospital and address my leg. When I arrived that evening after the rodeo, I encountered an infamous prison doctor, a bitter man who had been working with the prison for years. I informed him that I had broken my leg in the previous rodeo but had refused treatment at the time in order to participate in the last rodeo. With a look of disgust, he retorted, "If you're fit enough to go to that rodeo, you're fit enough to go down the walk." He then turned to the security and demanded, "Get this convict out of my office! Next."

Fortunately, I had those crutches and a bottle of Ibuprofen in the dorm. I nursed my leg over the next three months and gradually began walking again. I was determined to win this award, and no injury was too severe to deter me. I was willing to put in whatever amount of time exercising was necessary. Interestingly, Angola had an amateur boxing team. I observed that the only spiritual influence on the team was Islam. A thought occurred to me that I could join the boxing team and possibly share the gospel with some of the guys. Additionally, I could train with everyone and prepare for the rodeo. The only flaw in my plan was that I didn't know how to box. Nevertheless, I decided to join the team.

Walking into the gym, I noticed that the only thing white inside the building beside me was the floor. The boxers didn't appreciate my uninvited presence. Initially, they chose to ignore me. However, as I continued to show up, they decided to confront me in the ring, aiming to drive me away. They landed punches on every part of my body except the soles of my feet. Despite their efforts, I persisted in returning to the gym. I refused to give up. Eventually, the light heavyweight champ approached me and asked if I was one of those individuals who enjoyed pain.

I laughed and replied, "No." Seizing the opportunity, I shared my testimony and connected with him. Several months later, he embraced Jesus as his savior and enrolled in Bible College, responding to the calling on his life. Gradually, the other fighters also became my friends. I initiated Bible studies on the side of the ring. When Angola hosted an event featuring inmate boxers from other prisons across the state, I was invited to commence the show with a prayer. The gospel began to permeate every event within the prison. We even formed circles in the middle of the Rodeo arena to pray before the rodeo commenced. Typically, a Christian volunteer would lead us, but on one special day, Warden Cain decided to grant me the opportunity to address a sold-out arena with a microphone and open the event in prayer.

That same day, my chance to win the rodeo championship had finally arrived. God gave me grace to win every event I was assigned. I rode bulls, bareback horses, and won team events. I talked to reporters and shared my faith throughout the entire rodeo. When the final rodeo ended, everyone knew I had won it. The satisfaction of winning was so sweet.

A couple of months later, before the awards ceremony, a guy who wrote for the prison news magazine contacted me. He wanted to let me know before anyone else that some prison officials had stepped into the situation again and were taking my win away, giving it to someone else. I was so angry. This situation seemed so unfair. I felt helpless. I wanted to fight back, but it was me against some dangerous state officials. I asked God the question that never gets answered, "Why?"

Afterward, a question floated across my mind. "What's more important: this Rodeo championship or Jesus?" Suddenly, everything was back in proper perspective.

I knelt down and worshiped God. He remained good. He continued to be the one who rescued me when I didn't deserve it. He remained worthy of all my praise. Just because my situation didn't turn out how I wanted, it did not change the fact that God was good. Regardless of my present pain, I knew in my heart that the future would be better. I learned that my character was more important than a Championship buckle. This circumstance gave me the opportunity to honor the Lord in disappointing circumstances. Ironically, the inmate whom the officials were favoring approached me at the awards ceremony and said, "You won this rodeo. I'd give you this buckle if it didn't have my name on it. I had nothing to do with this situation." I reached over and hugged his neck. I told him that I have a relationship with Jesus, and they'll never be able to take that away from me. Then, I shared the gospel with him. I didn't have the buckle, but I walked away with a new friend.

Not long after I began my journey as a Christian cowboy, I also started my first classes at the Bible College. The Seminary sent some excellent professors to educate us. Most of them had a dual calling - not only to teach us but also to pastor us. Open discussions were common, with expected input from the student body. These men genuinely wanted us to succeed in our callings. Our only differences mainly revolved around the Baptism in the Spirit and our exuberant worship style. The focus on transforming the prison was so strong that our differences didn't distract us. Every day, I eagerly anticipated going to school. I made sure to sit directly in front of the lecturer because I didn't want to miss a single word.

After my first assignments, I got an A on each one. By the end of the semester, I had made all A's on my transcript. Afterwards, I received a letter from the Seminary informing me that I made the President's list. I wasn't trying to do that, but suddenly, I thought about setting a goal to achieve all A's for the next four years. I decided to graduate with a 4.0. I read in the book of Daniel that God gave an anointing to the four Hebrew children that caused them to excel in the academic training of their captive nation (Dan. 1:17). My general understanding of the Bible was if God did it for them, he would do it for me. He is no respecter of persons (Acts 10:34). For the next four years, I decided to trust him for academic excellence and success.

The demands of school and the challenges of prison often took a toll on my spiritual life. I struggled to prevent my academic studies from overshadowing my devotional practices. It's easy to convince oneself that listening to a formal lecture on the book of Isaiah is equivalent to personal devotional Bible reading – but I assure you, they are not the same. To withstand the fires of persecution, rejection, and misunderstanding, one must continually receive fresh manna from heaven. This spiritual nourishment is acquired through personal time spent with the Lord. Personal prayer and devotional reading are essential and nonnegotiable. No amount of seminary coursework can substitute for nurturing a personal relationship with the Lord.

During a challenging time in school, Assistant Warden Darrel Vannoy, who had been ascending the ranks in the prison administration, noticed me at the rodeo. Unaware of his identity, I was surprised when he approached me and pointed his finger at my chest. Addressing the person beside us, he remarked, "This is the guy I told you about. He's not afraid of anything." Then, turning to me, he asked, "Boy, do you want a job?" His demeanor suggested he held authority, so I replied, "Yes, sir." Inquiring further, he asked, "Are you a trustee?" I responded, "No, sir." Without hesitation, he declared, "You are now. Write me a letter, and I'll appoint you as a trustee to work for my brother on the Range Crew." With that, he turned and walked away. Puzzled, I turned to the person beside me and asked, "Who was that?" Proudly, he revealed that he was Warden Vannoy's brother. He explained that if I wrote to him, he would appoint me as a trustee to work as a cowboy on the Range Crew, assisting with the cattle operation on the farm.

In Angola, nobody attained trustee status unless they had served at least ten years—a practice deeply ingrained as an unwritten policy. Particularly for someone of my age, becoming a trustee was out of the question. The administration's assumption held firm: a young inmate with minimal time served would seize any chance to escape at the earliest opportunity. Additionally, prison policies barred me from being considered for trustee status due to being labeled as an escape risk, a consequence of my previous escape from Mississippi.

However, I saw in the Bible where Joseph obtained favor with the warden and became a trustee in prison, so I assumed that blessing was available to me, too (Gen. 39:21).

Warden Vannoy didn't respond immediately to my letter. Later, when I saw him, he explained that he wanted me to prioritize my education first. Then, he assured me, he would consider granting me trustee status and assigning me to work on the Range Crew. I sincerely believe that God had placed this on his heart. At that point in my life, completing my education became the most important goal. It became a defining moment for me. No longer would I quit when faced with challenges or frustrations. No longer would I abandon my efforts because something seemingly better came along. I was determined to persevere until I reached the finish line. From that moment forward, I was committed to seeing through whatever I started.

A couple of years later, I walked forward in a graduation ceremony to receive regionally accredited associate and bachelor's degrees. I was also the first inmate to achieve both degrees with a 4.0 average. With

Jesus in my heart, I felt there was nothing on Earth I couldn't do. After discussing my opportunity to become a cowboy with the head professor, I decided to accept Warden Vannoy's offer and become a trustee, transferring to the Range Crew. The Range Crew consisted of inmate cowboys who worked the cattle operation seven days a week. Since work started from sunup and lasted until after sundown, I saw an opportunity to take the gospel to them. I aimed to be a missionary to the cowboys. Soon after, I was transferred to Camp F, which housed the trustees working across the farm.

I cherished the time spent building relationships with these men and sharing with them about God's saving grace. Eventually, two well-known cowboys from the Range Crew answered the call on their lives. They left to join Bible College, seeking to become more effective servants for the Lord. Meanwhile, I roamed freely on horseback across the 18,000 acres, working with cows. Though the work was almost as demanding as fieldwork, at least there were no guns pointed at me.

Around this time, Warden Cain realized he had numerous seminary-trained graduates who could serve in ministry. He decided to pioneer something unprecedented. He revamped prison policies to include a role for inmate ministers. Essentially, he created a job title that would legally permit us to move throughout the prison, establishing churches, leading Bible studies, and counseling fellow inmates.

The head chaplain approached me about working for him as an inmate minister, and I accepted his offer, transferring back to the East Yard. He granted me access to the entire Main prison, allowing me to travel anywhere across the complex. However, I found myself spending most of my time in an office. Despite the comfort, I felt the need to be among people. My calling was to reach those who didn't know the Lord, and I also desired to impart the lessons I had learned to others through teaching.

I made the decision to create a role that would enable me to tutor Bible College students. My reasoning was that these men would likely become influencers, so by influencing them, I could potentially impact everyone under their guidance. After discussing the concept with the head professor, he promptly implemented it. My position was officially transitioned, eventually earning recognition as a Bible College tutor.

Since my departure, the school had expanded significantly. Remarkable prosocial changes were unfolding throughout the prison. Word had spread beyond the walls, and people on the outside had learned of the Christian movement within the prison, generously donating funds for the purchase of materials to construct chapels across the 18,000 acres. Inmates with construction skills were selected to erect beautiful chapels. Within a few years, worship buildings dotted the prison grounds, all at no expense to the state. The churches brimmed with inmates worshipping God, with services also led by seminary-trained inmates.

The benefits of being in school and becoming an inmate minister began attracting men with ulterior motives. Some of our professors were elderly and vulnerable, being pressured by unscrupulous individuals for better grades and reduced workload. Additionally, some inmates had formed a cheating network by sharing work. Placed in the midst of this chaos by the head professor, I was given a directive: "Fix it." Fortunately, the professors were pleased to have me on board and welcomed my assistance in their classes. I started by proctoring classes and grading assignments. Frequently, professors summoned me to the main office, entrusting me with administering exams due to scheduling conflicts preventing their presence.

In most prisons, a code exists that governs the inmate's social order. Sometimes, this list of rules is barbaric and fueled by egoism. At the top of every self-imposed list in prison is the expectation not to inform security (Thou shalt not rat!). Suddenly, I found myself thrust into a room full of prisoners, tasked with administering a major exam. Among them were men who held a deep love for the Lord, while others did not share the same devotion. I made it clear that I had no intention of involving security in the affairs of the Bible College. Instead, I informed them that if I caught anyone cheating, they would be brought before their church. This approach worked well for the believers. However, some inmates had obtained recommendations from unscrupulous pastors to gain admission to the school, leaving me with no church authority or body responsible for them.

Inevitably, I witnessed a man soliciting answers to exam questions from another inmate. Confronting them, I demanded they cease their actions. The individual, aware of the prison's unspoken code against informing security, wore a smug expression, thinking he had me cornered, especially since he didn't attend church. The pressure mounted as I realized that reporting the incident could tarnish my standing within the prison community. Caught between ignoring the situation or addressing it with higher authorities, I felt torn.

Later, as I collected the exams, I deliberated on what action to take. Then, a solution dawned on me. I retrieved two blank tests and traced their names onto each one. Being responsible for grading, I marked a conspicuous zero on both blank tests, attributing them to the respective individuals. During the next class, as I distributed the exams, I reached the two men in question. Firmly, I reminded them of my stance: "I said I wouldn't inform on you. You do the same." The most vocal individual promptly stood up, declaring in front of everyone that the test wasn't his. He rushed to the professor, who directed him to speak with me after class. However, he never followed through.

After serving in the ministry for several years, I contemplated seeking clemency from the outgoing governor. Throughout my tenure, I dedicated myself to transforming the prison culture. The administration recognized my efforts by honoring me for numerous significant achievements. Moreover, my disciplinary record remained exceptional, with only one instance of being sanctioned for a rule infraction. Unfortunately, a highly hostile and corrupt officer, who later ascended through the ranks of the prison administration, fabricated a report against me.

I was carrying Christian literature to the hospital when a captain, who disapproved of my actions, instructed an unscrupulous officer to sanction me and place me in administrative segregation. Consequently, the officer falsified paperwork, alleging that he had given me multiple direct verbal orders to return the literature to my dorm, which I purportedly refused. Fortunately, administrative segregation was at capacity, so I simply walked back to my dorm. A week later, I appeared in disciplinary court, where a lieutenant revoked my commissary privileges for two weeks. While the punishment wasn't overly severe, it tarnished my previously pristine disciplinary record, in which I took great pride.

Years after that incident, I compiled a portfolio showcasing all my accomplishments to submit to the governor. My intention was for her to recognize the disproportionate nature of my sentence and acknowledge the positive contributions I had made within Angola. Additionally, I planned to rally support from a network of individuals who believed in me and advocated for my release from prison. As I diligently assembled my package and connected with supporters, an embittered officer perceived my growing influence within the prison as a threat. Consequently, he made it his mission to tarnish my reputation and extinguish any hope of my eventual release. Fabricating a disciplinary report, he alleged that two confidential informants had disclosed that I was operating a brothel within my office. Ironically, I was summoned to the same lieutenant's office to be informed of these allegations.

When prisoners caught wind that this officer was aiming to confine me in a cell, they stepped up on my behalf, elucidating how this accusation was unfounded. People highlighted its implausibility based on timing and witness accounts. The lieutenant, having risen to the rank of captain, felt compelled to rectify this injustice, leading him to escort me to the individual responsible for the deceitful report penned against me years prior. This individual had since been promoted to assistant warden. He summoned the officer who authored the fraudulent report and attentively listened to the myriad inconsistencies and falsehoods presented. Not a single aspect of his narrative aligned or cohered logically.

I pointed directly at him and stated, "He's lying. It's as clear as day." The overseeing assistant warden shifted focus onto me, cautioning, "White boy, don't raise your voice in here. I'm about to show you who is running this prison!" He then turned to the captain who was advocating for me and instructed, "Hook him up!" This directive implied that the captain was to fabricate another damning report against me, intended to ensure my downfall.

These three individuals ultimately chose to dismiss the initial report. Subsequently, the captain drafted a disciplinary report accusing me of assaulting him. As a result, I was escorted to administrative lockdown and eventually transferred to Maximum Security lockdown in Camp J, housing the criminally insane. The officer presiding over the disciplinary court confided in me that he recognized my innocence regarding the alleged rule infraction, yet felt compelled to adhere to protocol.

I spent nearly a year in a solitary cell. Men had been housed in Camp J for so long that they lost their minds. Others arrived here with little of their minds left, embarking on this journey. I decided to hold a Bible study with the guy in the cell beside me. Consequently, I had the opportunity to lead him to the Lord and pray with him to receive Jesus as his savior. Others would listen as we discussed the lessons. Frequently, I was asked to teach English to the entire tier of cells. Those dishonest officers couldn't remove me from ministry because they were not the ones who called me to it in the first place.

While I was in lockdown, my mother spoke with a lawyer and arranged for him to visit me. She felt terrible about my situation and wanted to help in any way she could. Before being placed in lockdown, I had researched the laws relevant to my case and drafted a motion that I hoped to file in court. The laws clearly supported my position. My case had been mishandled during prosecution. I believed that if I could file this motion in court, I might persuade a judge to agree with my claims and secure my release from prison. When the lawyer, Rodney Baum, arrived, I still had the motion in my possession. I handed the document over to him. He assured me that he would promptly file my motion upon leaving the prison.

Unknown to me, when he left, he called my mother and informed her that it would take $10,000 for him to work on my case. After my mother handed over the money to him, I never saw or heard from him again. In fact, he never lifted a finger to help me. He didn't file a single document in court, conduct any legal research, or return my motion. When my mom tried to reach out to him by phone, he ignored her calls. When she finally managed to reach him, he bluntly stated, "If you want that money back, you will have to sue me in court. The money you paid me was a counseling fee." The lawyer had stolen the money from us. He knew we didn't have the resources to hire a lawyer to sue him because we had given everything to him. Essentially, he had robbed us.

Pastor Carl Everett and his cell group felt led to dedicate some time to prayer and fasting for my situation. They focused on my circumstances and petitioned the Lord to intervene and deliver me from the lockdown cell. Their prayers bore fruit when someone aware of my situation approached Warden Vannoy and informed him that I had been unjustly placed in lockdown. Prompted by this revelation, Warden Vannoy decided to personally investigate my case. After gathering sufficient information, he issued the order for my release.

I had anticipated that inmates who weren't walking with the Lord might give me a hard time about being sent to Maximum Security lockdown. Surprisingly, they connected with me instead. They shared a strong disdain for the corrupt individuals in the prison administration. To them, there was a clear struggle between the administration and themselves. In their eyes, I had become one of them, someone who suffered alongside them. Strangely, this newfound solidarity didn't diminish my credibility with the inmate population; rather, it enhanced it. I found myself able to speak into the lives of more inmates and empathize with the experiences they had endured.

Chapter 5

Becoming a Missionary

bout a year later, I attended a church service, and Warden Vannoy was present. He called me over and asked if I was a trustee. I said, "No sir." He told me, "I'll take care of that." That meant my custody status would change and more opportunities would be available throughout the prison. During this service, another assistant warden announced that all those with a college degree were going to take a test. This performance test would determine if you could become a teacher. They were formulating a plan to use us throughout the entire Department of Corrections as teachers and inmate ministers. The day came when several hundred of us took the test. Afterwards, twelve of us were called into a room.

We were informed that we had scored the highest among all who took the test. Additionally, we were told to select another prison because the administration planned to send us across the state to other facilities as missionary teachers. Louisiana had satellite prisons where we would hold positions in the Education department and the ministry. We were expected to enact the same change there that had occurred in Angola. They also tried to entice us with the promise of one dollar an hour for our work.

A few weeks later, I was instructed to pack my belongings as I was being transferred to Rayburn Correctional Center in Angie, Louisiana. Unfortunately, the only two people who knew that I was arriving for a job were on vacation. Upon my arrival, I informed the receiving officers who were processing me into the prison, "I'm an inmate minister. I've been sent here to start a church and work inside the Education department as a teacher. I'm here to help change the place and make a difference." However, they immediately assumed I was crazy, and consequently, they sent me to see the Mental Health staff.

When I arrived at the Mental Health department, my records happened to get switched with those of a guy who had serious mental problems. The lady evaluating me said, "Let's talk about this learning disability you have." I responded, "Ma'am, I have two college degrees and a 4.0 average. I have been sent here to be a teacher and an inmate minister." She quickly riffled through some pages and read a few lines. Looking up at me, she said, "It says here that you haven't been taking your medication." I couldn't help but laugh out loud. The situation struck me as humorous. However, I advise that if you find yourself in a similar situation with Mental Health officials questioning your medication, it's best not to laugh at them! Fortunately, the lady soon realized something was amiss. After checking my name and the name on the folder, she realized the mistake. Embarrassed, she said I was free to return to the dorm.

A couple of weeks later, Assistant Warden Wayne Cook and his wife, Education Director Andy Cook, returned from vacation and introduced themselves to me. This couple believed in education and spiritual formation, both being born-again Christians. Gradually, as they became aware of my capabilities and willingness to serve, they began entrusting me with responsibilities and empowering me to fulfill them. After being assigned a computer, I started teaching General Education Development (G.E.D.) classes and collaborating with professors who came to the prison to teach in an undergraduate program from River Parish Community College. Eventually, Warden Cook became so busy that he delegated the responsibility for overseeing the undergraduate program to me. I handled tasks such as scheduling classes, coordinating with professors, ordering textbooks, tracking students' grades and degree requirements, and collaborating on curriculum design with the professors. Additionally, I had the privilege of teaching classes in the absence of professors.

Eventually, I felt compelled to embark on a twenty-one-day liquid fast. Upon its completion, I approached Warden Cook to seek permission to establish a church within the newly constructed chapel. He enthusiastically supported the idea of a church plant and advised me to coordinate with Chaplain Mark Hollingsworth to arrange it. Following discussions with the chaplain, we agreed upon a date and time to commence the endeavor

In the interim, I wandered the prison yard, engaged in prayer, pondering how to establish a church within the confines of this institution. A significant concern loomed regarding the absence of a music team. As I traversed, contemplating the logistical challenge of conducting a church service sans music, I was approached by an individual who had heard of my role as an inmate minister. Confirming this, he expressed a dilemma: he and a group of fellow inmates had formed a Christian band utilizing the prison's musical equipment, but lacked a venue to perform. Grinning, I responded, "I believe I may be able to assist you gentlemen."

Word began to circulate throughout the prison about the impending launch of the new inmate minister's church. Another individual, confined to a wheelchair, approached me expressing a desire to contribute. He stated, "I may not be able to do much physically, being stuck in this wheelchair, but I can assist in writing letters to every person in the prison." Accompanied by three willing companions, they volunteered to sit down with pen and paper, diligently crafting handwritten invitations to each inmate.

Subsequently, I was summoned to the office of the mental health professional I had previously encountered. She acknowledged being aware of the forthcoming church plant and conveyed her intention to recommend that the inmates she counseled engage with me and join the ministry I was establishing. Furthermore, she expressed her plan to bring her staff along to attend the inaugural service.

One of the most peculiar encounters I experienced in relation to the church plant involved a witch who led a coven within the prison. At Rayburn Correctional Center, there was an approved Wiccan group that convened every Thursday evening. During their gatherings, they engaged in spell casting and spirit channeling. The leader of this coven approached me upon hearing about my initiative to start a nondenominational church. Surprisingly, he expressed support for the idea and expressed intentions to bring the entire Wiccan community to listen to my preaching.

The invitation letters for the inaugural service were penned and dispatched to every inmate in the general population. Soon after, we eagerly opened the doors to the chapel. Security signaled the start of the service with a whistle blast, granting permission for the population to attend. As the music concluded and I positioned myself behind the pulpit, I couldn't help but observe the presence of every witch in the prison, alongside the Mental Health workers and members of the Classification department. It was heartening to see inmates from every unit gather for the service.

I had resolved to preach the exclusivity of the cross. Jesus wasn't merely a way among many ways. He was the only way to heaven. He wasn't one truth among many truths. He was the truth. He wasn't just a life among many lives to emulate. He was the sole life that provided access to the Father. I poured my heart into the sermon and delivered it with fervor. I anticipated sparks to fly when the witches and Muslims in the audience heard the message; however, they sat there, listened intently, and approached me after the service, shaking my hand.

The head witch said, "Alex that was pretty good. We'll all be back next week." I was dumbfounded. Initially, I couldn't comprehend why they were at ease listening to that message. Later, it dawned on me— they believed in relativism. In other words, what was true for me was true for me, but what was true for them was true for them. Truth was relative, not absolute, so there was nothing to be offended over. What held true for Alex didn't necessarily hold true for the witches. In their perspective, both viewpoints were valid.

I continued preaching the exclusivity of Jesus's cross the next week and issued the altar call. Astonishingly, one of the witches stood up and walked down the aisle to repent and receive Jesus as his Lord and Savior. I held hands with him and prayed with him to accept Jesus. Afterwards, I announced that those who had been saved during the service would be baptized the following week. Following counseling with the individual, I became convinced that he genuinely believed Jesus died for his sins. He expressed his desire to be forgiven for his sins, so I scheduled him for baptism.

Every witch in the prison attended the next service to support his decision to get baptized. During the ceremony, as I was about to baptize him, a sudden insight struck me. Holding him in the baptismal pool, I asked, "Do you believe that Jesus is the only way a person can be saved?" He replied, "Yes." I continued, "Do you believe that he died for your sins and the sins of the entire world?" Again, he affirmed, "Yes." Then, I asked, "Do you believe that he was resurrected from the dead for your justification?" Once more, he said, "Yes." It was at this moment that the insight dawned on me. I asked, "Do you renounce your ties and affiliation with the occult and every counter belief system?" His answer came without hesitation, "Yes, I do." I said, "With that confession, I baptized you in the name of the Father, and the Son, and the Holy Spirit!" And I immersed him.

The witches in the crowd became furious. It was as if a spell had been broken. Suddenly, they realized the essence of my message: it wasn't about merging or equalizing belief systems, but rather about rejecting and separating from the old system of thought. It boiled down to Jesus and only Jesus for salvation. The witches convened and approached me at the front of the chapel, eager to hear me clarify what I had just said and done.

I explained that the Bible teaches that faith in Jesus is the sole path to entering heaven. It requires a person to turn from sin through repentance and place trust in the finished work of Calvary; nothing else suffices for salvation. In no uncertain terms, the head witch declared that if that's what I believed and taught, then we were at war with each other. Over the next several months, the witches slandered me and attempted to turn the prison population against me. They also informed me that they were praying for my failure. (Praying to whom? I wondered.) Frequently, they sent me letters adorned with symbols and curses. I would fold them up and keep them in my Bible, almost like trophies.

During those months of slander, the witches persisted in attending my services to hear firsthand what I was preaching. Consequently, I occasionally led one of them to the Lord. In one service, I utilized a PowerPoint presentation to outline the Bible's prohibition against the practice of witchcraft. This deeply upset the witches. Their attempts to turn people against me inadvertently piqued the interest of the inmate population, prompting them to attend the services to understand the controversy. Eventually, the leader of the witches decided it would be best for them to avoid my services altogether.

The witches regularly indulged in drug use, incorporating it into their rituals and services. The ringleader, who persistently caused me trouble, enlisted his father's help in smuggling synthetic marijuana into the prison. Known on the streets as K-2, MoJo, or Spice, these substances were discreetly brought in. Utilizing the prison telephone and an approved email system, he coordinated with his father on the logistics of the drug drops. However, prison officials became aware of their activities and began monitoring their conversations and correspondence. Consequently, the administration initiated an operation to apprehend them. Swiftly, they arrested the ringleader's father. Under interrogation, the ringleader ultimately confessed, implicating his father in the process.

The same evening as the arrest, the five o'clock televised news aired a comprehensive segment detailing the events and revealing the individual who informed on his father. The inmate population reacted with fury. They turned against the practitioners of Wicca, viewing them as traitors. In the eyes of the average inmate, witches were considered informants. Prison officials responded by placing the leader of the Wiccan group on administrative lockdown. Eventually, Wiccan meetings ceased altogether. Just as my conflict with the Wiccans concluded, I felt compelled to delve into teaching about the distinctions between Christianity and Islam. I wondered, what harm could that possibly cause?

Using PowerPoint, I meticulously detailed to my congregation the disparities between Christianity and Islam. I emphasized that in Islam, Jesus is regarded as merely a human being, while in Christianity, and he is believed to be the incarnation of God. Furthermore, Islam denies the concept of the Trinity, which is fundamental to Christianity, asserting that God is Father, Son, and Holy Spirit.

Occasionally, certain individuals attended my services with the sole intention of eavesdropping, seeking material they could exploit to sow discord. In this instance, they happened to be present during my comparison of Islam and Christianity. Without delay, they departed and proceeded to inform members of the Muslim community that I was speaking against Islam.

The following day, the inmate Imam sought me out. He approached with an accusatory point of his index finger and said, "Hey man, I heard you've been speaking against Islam." I offered a partial defense, stating,

"No, I didn't speak against Islam. I simply highlighted the disparities between Christianity and Islam. I concluded that we worship different deities." His anger flared, retorting, "You have no right to disrespect the Quran in any manner." Ironically, amidst his escalating fury, he asserted, "We are peaceful people!" I replied, "Well brother, be peaceful." About that time, an officer started walking our way, so he said, "Don't speak against Islam again or face consequences! We'll continue this conversation later."

As I reflected on the situation, I began preparing for my next service. I did what any Spirit filled believer would do in that situation. I taught the next service on the distinctions between Christianity and Islam. Before news of the service could reach the Imam, an unexpected turn of events unfolded. The Imam shared a cell with an individual whose sister had been a victim of rape. During their conversation, she made the decision to disclose the identity of her assailant, a revelation that stunned her brother — it was none other than the Imam who had threatened me.

Fueled by anger and vengeance, the brother immediately sought out the Imam and attempted to take his life. Security intervened just in time to prevent a tragedy, and the Imam was swiftly transferred to another correctional facility and placed under protective custody.

The Islamic community convened following the incident and conducted an election. They elected a replacement whom I found to be compatible. Upon learning that I was educating about the distinctions between Islam and Christianity, the community sought guidance from the new Imam regarding my presence. He reassured them that I was acceptable. "What Alex believes applies to Alex. However, what we believe applies to us." They all agreed, and I never had another problem with the Islamic community.

Amidst these ongoing battles, Warden Cook approached me one day with a proposition: to establish a correspondence program under the River Parish Community College undergraduate program. This initiative aimed to deliver courses necessary for a Certificate of General Studies to inmates in various facilities across the state. I was assigned the responsibility of drafting an administrative guide along with a textbook, which would be distributed electronically to the directors of prison education. Professionals holding degree credentials were consulted to review and approve my work. Subsequently, I packaged the textbooks and dispatched them via prison transportation vehicles to satellite prisons across Louisiana.

My responsibilities also included creating registration forms and sending them to prisons across the state via Warden Cook, establishing a database, forwarding the registration forms to River Parish Community College through Warden Cook, managing the sending, receiving, grading, and tracking of all assignments and degree requirements, and ensuring professors were kept informed of pertinent information. Following the success of these efforts, Warden Cook proposed the creation of a paralegal program. Initially, his plan involved bringing lawyers into the prison to teach courses onsite, followed by the development of a correspondence program akin to the previous initiative. However, we encountered our first challenge when faced with a shortage of textbooks. Given the high cost of law books, Warden Cook suggested that we undertake the task of writing them ourselves.

We convened with an inmate counsel who possessed an impressive understanding of the law, rivaling that of many trial lawyers in Louisiana. Essentially functioning as an accredited paralegal, he served as an inmate advocate, assisting individuals with their criminal cases post-incarceration. Warden Cook's proposal entailed the counsel and me co-authoring an Introduction to Paralegal Studies textbook, with oversight from a lawyer brought in to validate our work. To fund the printing of the book, Warden Cook devised a plan to secure a loan from an inmate organization operating a cake-selling venture in the visiting area. Subsequently, the textbook would be printed, collated, and distributed to other prisons. Profits from sales would then reimburse the inmate organization and provide funding for subsequent book projects. Ultimately, we successfully executed this process four times.

Certain inmates, aware of my involvement in these projects without receiving due recognition, criticized me, suggesting that I was allowing myself to be exploited. Little did they know, months prior, Warden Cook had approached me with an opportunity to pursue a master's degree. One evening, he contacted me and proposed joining a Master of Arts program facilitated by Global University, an Assemblies of God University located in Springfield, Missouri. Representatives from the university visited Louisiana to assess the facility and officially launch the program. The only hurdle was the substantial financial requirement to complete the degree. With only one thousand dollars to my name, Warden Cook assured me that my savings would be sufficient to commence the program. However, I recognized the need for many more thousands to reach the finish line. My aspiration was to accumulate enough funds over time to afford legal representation and potentially reduce my sentence.

By faith, I handed over the money to get started in the program. I decided to trust God for the rest. One evening, while I was helping Warden Cook in his office, a check fell out of his mail for ten thousand dollars. A Christian businessman had heard about the master's program and felt led to donate some money for our continued education. These types of financial miracles continued until I finished my first Master of Art degree. During the program, I set the same lofty goal as I had in the undergraduate program: to finish with a consistent A average. When I finished my last master's class, I had achieved it. As a result, I was invited to join Delta Epsilon Tau's International Honors Society. I became the first inmate in the Louisiana system to obtain a regionally accredited master's degree.

The University's staff was so excited that they decided to fly to Louisiana and hold a graduation ceremony inside the prison for me. My graduation was also a first for the school. They had never had a prisoner obtain a postgraduate degree from them before. The prison staff graciously allowed Global to award me with a Master's robe, a cape, and the degree. They also filmed the ceremony and interviewed me. Pictures of my church service and a baptism were included in the production. Global University sent the video all over the world. Not long after graduation, Warden Cook asked if I'd like to pursue a Master of Divinity (M-Div). I gladly said yes. He contacted the university and set up the program in the prison. Immediately, I began working toward my second master's degree.

During all this time, I had also been working toward an Associate in General Studies degree with River Parish Community College. I only needed a little over sixty hours to obtain the degree; however, I took every class that was offered (except the ones that I taught). In order to maintain academic integrity due to my high level of involvement in the school, my class participation and grades were overseen by the education director. I ended up completing over one hundred and twenty hours for this sixty hour degree. I thought that one day, when I am free, I may be able to use the extra areas of concentration to pursue another degree in that field. Eventually, the River Parish staff came and presented me with my second Associate degree with honors. I achieved a 4.0 GPA.

I debated whether to mention that during my time in incarceration, I also acquired a TCA from North Shore Technical College in Small Engines and a certificate from the Louisiana Technical College in Graphic Communications. On the surface, these two achievements may not seem like spiritual milestones, but I believe it's crucial to recall that the Apostle Paul himself was a Tentmaker. There were occasions when he had to labor and sustain himself when the ministry couldn't provide for him. Prisoners require avenues to cultivate trade skills for a trade. When a man or woman is released from prison, it is vital that they are employed as soon as possible. Any opportunity while incarcerated to learn a trade to help them obtain employment when released is important. Every chance I get, I encourage prisoners to avail themselves to vocational opportunities offered in prison.

While the inmate counsel and I were working on the paralegal books mentioned earlier, a lawyer who was overseeing one of the projects asked me a personal question about my court case. Before this question from the lawyer, I had never asked him for anything. I did not even ask him for the time of day. I simply helped him in any way I could. My objective was to serve him as if I were doing it for the Lord. In answer to his question, I shared my experience and what happened in my criminal case. He was intrigued by the story, so he asked me more questions. When the questioning was over, he said, "Alex, the courts can't do that to you. I'm going to fix your situation." He walked out of that prison, and within twenty-four hours, Warden Cook called me to the administration building where he worked.

He stood up and reached across the desk, handing me a new document containing a recalculation of my time, now including a parole date in five years. With a handshake, he said, "Congratulations Alex, it looks like you have a chance to get out of prison." I went from possibly facing a lifetime behind bars to having a potential release in just a few years.

When the lawyer returned for his next visit, I inquired about the cost of his assistance. Surprisingly, he insisted I didn't owe him anything. Ironically, within a few years, he emerged as Louisiana's leading authority on parole and pardons. In my case, he was well-versed in a piece of legislation passed in the 1980s, which affected a mere forty prisoners out of forty thousand. Fortunately, I happened to be one of them. He didn't require court intervention; instead, he resolved my situation by leveraging his connections within the Department of Corrections.

Chapter 6

Returning to Angola

fter three years and eight months of missionary work at Rayburn, I transferred back to Angola. I was at the end of my Master of Divinity program, needing to finalize my degree by composing a Master's thesis. I meticulously crafted the right research question and dedicated myself to completing the project. Upon completing my thesis, titled "The Cultural Evolution of the Louisiana State Penitentiary," I submitted it for review. The university staff expressed great satisfaction with my work. The A grade I received for my thesis further solidified my consistent A average throughout my second postgraduate degree. Once again, the staff from Global University flew to Louisiana and organized another graduation ceremony for me. I was once again honored by Delta Epsilon Tau's International Honors Society, and Global's staff presented me with another Master's cape, conferring upon me a Master of Divinity degree.

The leaders at Global University were impressed not only by my academic achievements but also by my dedication to ministry. As a result, they made the decision to grant me a scholarship for a regionally accredited Doctorate in Ministry degree. Chaplain Jim Rentz, a revered figure with over sixty years of service to God as an Assemblies of God minister, personally delivered this exciting news. His guidance and support had been instrumental in my ministry journey, particularly within the prison system

The university staff collaborated with the prison administration to initiate the program. Under the direction of the head chaplain, Ricky Sharkey, I was granted access to the seminary library and a computer designated for Bible College students. With these resources at my disposal, I had everything necessary to successfully complete the degree program.

When I returned to Angola, the prison officials were pleased with my years of success at Rayburn Correctional Center. I had reached ten percent of the prison population and had them attending church regularly. Over three hundred of my church members returned home.

Occasionally, I heard about many of my fellow inmates' success in adapting to life outside prison. Some became sign language interpreters, businessmen, and laborers. By God's grace, I never heard of any of them returning to prison. In addition, inmates all over the state had been positively influenced by the educational programs I helped create and run. The prison staff gave me the option to hold a trustee job and serve as an inmate minister simultaneously. I accepted the offer and became a bi-vocational minister for the prison.

I began breaking horses for Angola's Equine Training Center as I completed my M-Div and worked on my thesis. Eventually, when I started my D-min, the Row Crop operation required an office clerk. This operation oversaw all planting and harvesting activities across Angola's 18,000 acres of vegetable, cotton, and soybean fields. I accepted the position and was provided with a well-equipped office, including a computer. My supervisor allowed me to use the computer for my schoolwork once my clerical duties were fulfilled. During crop harvests, the entire crew often worked from six in the morning until three o'clock the following morning. These long hours provided me with uninterrupted time to write for hours in a comfortable, air-conditioned environment— a luxury not available elsewhere in the prison.

During this period, I completed all my required, elective, and research-specific classes for my doctorate. Then, I took on the most significant writing assignment of my academic journey. I needed to formulate a question statement and commence research for my dissertation. My inquiry was straightforward yet profound: "Do individuals sentenced to life in prison without the possibility of parole in the Louisiana State Penitentiary shed their criminal mindset and become capable of responsible citizenship?" This task drew upon the culmination of my educational experiences, both academically and spiritually, preparing me to tackle it head-on. I began my research journey in pursuit of answers.

Around this time, New Orleans Baptist Theological Seminary initiated a regionally accredited Master's program within the prison. Seeking to enroll, I approached the head chaplain. Surprisingly, he was resistant, believing I already possessed sufficient education. However, I was convinced otherwise. I couldn't fathom letting such an opportunity slip away. Persistently, I advocated for my enrollment until he relented, allowing me to join approximately forty other inmates in the program.

Over time, the chaplain grew more receptive to my presence as I dedicated hours to tutoring struggling peers. Through perseverance and, perhaps, by the grace of God, I resolved to pursue my doctoral dissertation concurrently with my third master's degree.

During this phase of my life, I underwent an experience reminiscent of the character portrayed in the oldest book of the Bible, Job. I endured the loss of my entire immediate family. It commenced with the passing of my biological father, a man I would never have the chance to know. Shortly after receiving this devastating news, I was summoned to make a call home – a dreaded notification for any prisoner. It was a clear indication that something tragic had occurred. As anticipated, I learned that my beloved mother, my greatest supporter, had unexpectedly passed away. Four months elapsed before another blow struck: the loss of my grandmother. Then, four months later, my grandfather followed. Within the span of a year, I found myself utterly alone, awakening to a world devoid of familial presence. Regrettably, the state of Louisiana refused to transport me to the funerals, citing their location in Mississippi. Despite the habit I had formed of phoning home on weekends, I would now confront the stark reality of picking up the prison phone only to find no one on the other end to receive the call. It was at this juncture that I truly began to rely entirely on the Lord.

I continued to save money over the years. As an inmate minister, I earned twenty cents an hour. During my missionary trip, my involvement in the education department bumped my hourly wage to seventy-five cents for about two years. Throughout this time, I remained committed to tithing and giving offerings to ministries and churches that had impacted my life. Remarkably, God orchestrated financial miracles, providing for my needs and allowing me to enjoy things that the prison couldn't offer.

Upon my return to Angola, I decided to invest some money with another prisoner and venture into building kitchen table sets to sell at the Angola rodeo. Utilizing the prison's hobby shop, where inmates could craft and sell their creations for profit, proved to be a fruitful decision. The Lord blessed this endeavor, enabling me to save exponentially more than before. I was resolute in ensuring I had enough funds to acquire what I needed once the Lord granted me freedom from prison.

Eventually, I saved ten thousand dollars. The lawyer who had previously helped me had made quite a name for himself representing prisoners in parole and pardon hearings. He was undoubtedly the best. As a result, he charged ten thousand dollars to represent a client. Louisiana had a reputation for being tough on crime, and very few people were granted parole through their system. This lawyer had a great success rate in getting his clients approved for parole. I wrestled with the idea of giving him my ten thousand dollars that I had saved. If I go before the parole board by myself, I could use my money to get the things I need when I'm released, but if I go before the parole board by myself, I could easily be denied. Should I pay him to represent me? Or should I go in there by myself? I thought to myself that if I didn't try everything in my power, I may regret it for years to come.

As I prayed about this situation, the lawyer sent a message to me in prison. He said, "Let me know when you get within a year of your hearing. I want to represent you." I was overwhelmed by the goodness of God. The best lawyer in the business was going to represent me free of charge on one of the most hostile parole boards in America. One of the first things we discussed was the need for my family to travel to the prison for the hearing. He explained that the board must see that your family has your back. In fact, he wanted to seat them directly behind me in the hearing to convey the picture that they were literally behind me. If a person gets out of prison, he or she needs people to help them transition back into society. Considering I lost my family, what was I to do?

While I was praying through this situation, I received a letter from a friend of mine from high school. I hadn't seen Crystal in over twenty years. She had become friends with my grandfather, who often spoke about his grandson, though my name never surfaced in their conversations. One day, he mentioned me, and she finally asked, "What is your grandson's name? I hear you mention him often, but I haven't caught his name." He told her, "Alex Hennis." She was excited because she remembered our friendship in school. She asked him for my address, but he failed to get it to her. After he passed away, she decided to research and find out how to contact me. Eventually, she obtained my address and wrote to me. We began corresponding over the next few months. She was a Christian who loved the Lord. The rodeo was approaching, so she decided to make the trip from Mississippi to Louisiana to watch the rodeo and visit with me. It was such a blessing to see her after all those years.

Crystal was a stunning girl back in school. When I caught sight of her again, I was struck by how she hadn't seemed to age a day. She possessed a timeless beauty that belied her years. We kept in touch through letters and phone calls, and eventually, I put in a request to have her added to my visiting list at the prison. It took some effort, but eventually, she was approved. Our first visit fell on February 14th, and if I didn't know any better, I'd say it felt like divine intervention. Interestingly, neither of us had been seeking a relationship at the time. But over the ensuing years, that's precisely what blossomed between us. We fell deeply in love, and Crystal became an incredibly supportive presence in my life.

During one of our visits, she confided in me that she felt the Lord had revealed I was meant to be her husband. It brought to mind the story of Adam and Eve in the garden—Adam hadn't been actively searching for a partner, yet God brought Eve to him. Similarly, I couldn't deny that Crystal felt like the Eve meant for me, brought into my life by the Lord.

I confided in Crystal about my dilemma regarding the necessity of having family members present at my parole hearing. After praying about it, she later said to me, "Alex, I'm going to rent a van and gather all my close family members to travel with me to Angola for your hearing. We're going to be your family." It was an answer to my prayers. I wouldn't have to face the hearing alone.

During the hearing, the prison officials utilized a television camera to transmit those of us undergoing hearings to Baton Rouge, where the parole board members convened. Conversely, the board members were transmitted into the prison where we were. Pastor Carl Everett made the decision to accompany his wife and some members of their cell group to Baton Rouge for the hearing. They would be present with the parole board members, offering prayers that God would move their hearts to grant me mercy.

Before my hearing, the day arrived when I completed my dissertation. I submitted the final copy for review, and the university flew in the professors who comprised my committee from Missouri to Louisiana for my defense hearing. Standing before these esteemed men, arguably some of the brightest minds I had encountered, I defended my dissertation for six hours. At the conclusion, they extended their hands to welcome me into their ranks. They now considered me one of them. I had earned the title of Dr. Alex Hennis. This marked a historic moment in Louisiana's prison history, as I became the first inmate to attain a regionally accredited doctorate degree.

For a couple of years, I held onto the hope of completing my doctorate before my parole hearing. I aimed to obtain a copy of my degree to include it in the portfolio of achievements my lawyer and I were compiling for submission to the parole board. However, several months passed after my Oral Dissertation Defense Hearing, and I hadn't received any updates from the university. With the date of my parole hearing drawing near, I began to feel anxious. Yet, as it turned out, things didn't unfold as I had envisioned. God had something even greater in store.

Global reached out to the prison, seeking permission to organize a graduation ceremony just three days before my hearing. Remarkably, three of the professors scheduled to attend the ceremony also intended to stay for my parole hearing. Their commitment went beyond academic support; they were willing to advocate for my release and convey to the parole board their belief in my potential.

About a year before my graduation, a surprising turn of events occurred at Angola. Warden Burl Cain, after twenty-five years of service, announced his retirement. This prompted the Secretary of Corrections to begin the search for his successor. After careful consideration, the Louisiana Department of Corrections appointed Warden Darrel Vannoy as the new head of Angola. Interestingly, the head warden's presence was required at each parole hearing, and Warden Vannoy had been acquainted with me for nearly the entirety of my incarceration. He was intimately familiar with all my accomplishments, and, most importantly, he had unwavering faith in me.

In another turn of events, the assistant warden who previously fabricated reports against me and had me locked in a cell was arrested in connection with a drug smuggling operation inside the prison. The lies he wrote against my character would not be used against me. In addition, he would not be present at the hearing to speak against me. Circumstances were shifting in my favor.

Three days before my hearing, Warden Vannoy and Chaplain Ricky Sharkey graciously facilitated another graduation for me. The administration's generosity extended to permitting me to invite close friends from various sections of the prison, as well as opening attendance to the general population. Furthermore, they arranged for the entire ceremony to be broadcasted on the prison TV channel, allowing the entire prison community to witness the event. The Global staff arrived with a doctoral robe, a cape, and my degree. Following the professors' administration of the graduation ceremony and the conferral of my degree, I delivered a speech to the assembled audience.

As a result of the graduation, a significant wave of positive momentum propelled me into my hearing. Three days later, the awaited moment arrived: my parole hearing. Chaplain Jim Rentz arrived accompanied by members of Global's staff. Among them were three esteemed professors: Dr. Randy Hedlun, the Dean of Graduate Studies; Dr. David DeGarmo, the Provost; and Dr. Clinton Caszatt, the Chairman of my Dissertation Committee, all prepared to advocate on my behalf.

As the proceedings began, Crystal entered the room with a group of seventeen individuals trailing behind her. While I recognized all of her family members, the final person caught me by surprise. Approaching me, Crystal introduced him, saying, "Alex, this is James. He's the brother you never knew you had."

After my father divorced my mother, he remarried and had two boys and a girl. Unbeknownst to me, they existed, but they eventually discovered information about my existence. James and his sister, Jane, had always harbored a desire to reach out to me but were unsure how I would receive them or if I would even want to connect with them. Secretly, they pondered these thoughts, wondering about the possibility of forming a relationship. Through a fortuitous turn of events, Crystal managed to locate James and explained my circumstances to him. He made the decision to journey to Angola to offer his support for my parole endeavors. It felt like a divine intervention, as God seemed to be restoring a family to me. Upon meeting James and Jane, I not only liked them, but I also felt a profound love for them and was overjoyed to welcome them into my life.

Once the hearing officially commenced, Warden Vannoy chose to interject himself into the meeting just as the board members were preparing to question me. He stated, "Board members, I feel it necessary to inform you all before we proceed that this inmate recently made history. Three days ago, he attained a regionally accredited doctorate degree. This marks the first instance in Louisiana's history where an inmate has achieved such a feat. Furthermore, he has served this prison admirably and has never caused any trouble under my watch." The Chairman of the Board leaned back, visibly surprised, and turned to me, asking, "Well, we've never encountered a situation like this before. Dr. Hennis, are you ready to begin?" I replied, "Yes, sir." Over the next several minutes, I faced a barrage of questions. I approached each query with humility, taking full responsibility for my actions and providing truthful responses. Subsequently, an opportunity arose for someone to advocate on my behalf.

Even though I had the right to present three speakers on my behalf, my lawyer suggested we only go with one. Keep in mind, this individual is the foremost authority on pardons and parole in the state of Louisiana. I responded, "Sure. What's your legal reasoning?" He smiled and replied, "They're hungry." I must have looked puzzled. He clarified, "As a courtesy, we aren't going to detain the board members from breaking for lunch." This advice came from the top lawyer in the state. I saw no reason to contest his suggestion. We would offer one speaker and allow the board to reach their decision.

Dr. Randy Hedlun was granted the floor, and his speech was nothing short of captivating. Among his words, a few stood out and remain etched in my memory: "Ladies and Gentlemen, we have a body of research from Alex that spans over ten years and reflects his intimate thinking processes. I can testify that he is no longer the same man who entered this prison system. I stake my academic authority on it. Furthermore, I'll stake my academic career on it. If you will allow him to go free, we will hire him as a professor." These words reverberated throughout the entire room. Following that speech, there was no need for another speaker.

After Dr. Hedlun concluded his speech and resumed his seat, the chairman announced his readiness to conduct a vote among the board members. Three individuals held my fate in their hands: freedom or lifelong imprisonment. Following each member's expression of thoughts and their votes, the chairman tallied two in favor of my release. In his closing statement, he declared, "Dr. Hennis, I also vote to grant you freedom. We find no justification to prolong your incarceration." A collective sigh of relief swept through the room. While I comprehended the outcome intellectually, the full emotional impact hadn't yet struck me. It felt as though I were observing the proceedings unfold like a scene from a television program. Gradually, over the ensuing hours, the reality sunk in bit by bit: this chapter of my life was finally drawing to a close.

The word quickly spread across the prison that I was granted release. The atmosphere became festive. Men realized that if God did it for me, He would do it for them too. One guy confided in me and said, "Bro, it would have been the end of the world for us if you didn't make it." I asked, "Why?" He replied, "If you can't make it past the board with all your accomplishments, there's no way any of us can!" We shared a good laugh, and I began counting down the days until the administration processed my paperwork and released me. Strangely, the days turned into weeks. The weeks turned into months.

Finally, after three months, I was informed of the day when someone could pick me up at the front gate. I had packed some bags with all my possessions that I would be taking with me. After all these years, Pastor

Carl Everett was waiting at the front gate to pick me up. Scott Holmes, the District Superintendent over Louisiana's Assemblies of God churches, was prepared to allow me to speak the following week at their gathering of church leaders from across the state. We had become friends after successfully planting an Assemblies of God church inside the prison, which was pastored by an inmate. Incredible days were ahead.

Mrs. Ruth Graham, Billy Graham's youngest daughter, and her dear friend Mary Brandes, daughter of Linton Tibbetts who helped develop the Cayman Islands, had a ministry trip planned for me as well. I had met Mrs. Graham and Mrs. Brandes years earlier. Both ladies were intrigued by the move of God that was occurring inside the prison. I had the opportunity to get to know them both and pray with them. Mrs. Brandes wrote her contact information on a small piece of paper, and at the top, she wrote, "Promissory note for a trip to the Cayman Islands." She said, "Once you are free, you contact me. Bring this piece of paper and redeem it. My husband and I will fly you to the Cayman Islands for a ministry trip." She also mentioned that her son, Senator Jeff Brandes of Florida, would assist me with any travel document-related issues I might encounter. You could sense her deep desire to help the native people of the Caymans.

One year, I won a Rodeo Buckle and felt compelled to give it to Mrs. Graham during one of her visits to the prison. Once she returned home, she placed it in her office, and every time she glanced at it, she prayed for me. However, during each subsequent visit to the prison, she would bring the trophy buckle with her and attempt to return it to me. After she shared the story about praying for me each time she saw it, I told her,

"There was no way on earth that I would take that buckle back!"

Mrs. Ruth and Mrs. Mary both have a heart for the people in the Cayman Islands and eagerly anticipated the day when we could minister to them together. Finally, the day I had dreamed about had arrived. After 25 consecutive years of imprisonment, I was about to step outside the prison as a free man and begin my new life. Just before I could take that first step to freedom, a Mississippi State Trooper arrived at the front gate. As I was about to step through the gate to freedom, he said, "Alex, you will have to come with me." Astonished, I asked, "Why?" He replied, "You owe Mississippi time from nearly thirty years ago when you were a kid." Due to the lack of records, they were bringing me back to start over the sentence that was handed to Louisiana over twenty-five years ago.

Chapter 7

Shanghaied to Mississippi

e drove quickly across the state line into Mississippi. I was handed over to the Central Mississippi Correctional Facility (C.M.C.F.) for processing into the Department of Corrections. Initially, no one knew what to do with me. There were no computers or internet in the Mississippi Department of Corrections (M.D.O.C.) when I got into trouble. No electronic files existed on me. The paperwork they had was archived in a cardboard box buried in a warehouse somewhere.

I overheard a conversation among members of the classification department. One woman suggested that since there was nothing in the computer system except that my sentence was officially discharged over ten years ago, they should release me. Another woman said, "I don't want to be bothered with all that paperwork. I'm just gon'na make him start it over." That meant I would have to start a new ten-year sentence beginning the day the State Trooper picked me up.

To make matters worse, I was taken to see a psychiatrist. This man was undoubtedly one of the most hateful and sadistic individuals I had encountered in all my years of imprisonment. He asked me a series of questions that had no relevance to my mental health. Each question seemed more rhetorical in nature, intended to debase me while asserting his superiority in a godlike fashion. I quickly realized he was not there to assess my mental state. For whatever reason, he had a sadistic agenda to pursue.

He persistently attempted to offer me medication to address issues that I did not have. Eventually, he asked if I were suicidal. Calmly, I responded, "No sir." He then inquired if I ever thought about hurting myself. I calmly reassured him that I had no desire to hurt myself. However, with a smug look on his face, he stated, "I have to place you on suicide watch to be sure. We can't have you hurting yourself."

I remained calm, yet I carefully pleaded with the man not to put me on suicide watch, emphasizing that I had no desire to hurt myself. Upon witnessing the discomfort in my expression at the thought of being placed on suicide watch, he displayed an intense look of satisfaction.

When the administration places a prisoner on suicide watch, they strip him naked and confine him in a cell under constant supervision. Nothing is permitted in the cell: no clothes, no Bible, no toothbrush, no toothpaste, and no bed linen—absolutely nothing. It is the worst form of dehumanization and legal torture that a prisoner can experience. They strip away not only your clothes but also your dignity. Observation is carried out via camera or by an officer walking by every 15 minutes, sometimes both.

Immediately following our conversation, I was escorted to a cell, stripped of all my clothes, and literally thrown inside naked. The sound of the steel door slamming shut behind me is something one can never forget.

Once inside, I felt a blast of cold air blowing over me. The cell was equipped with an air conditioner, and it was set to its highest level. As I mentioned earlier, the cell was constructed of concrete with a steel door. The window, which faced the exterior of the building, was coated with a thick layer of black substance, rendering it impossible to see outside.

On the bare floor, I began pacing back and forth in the confines of that small cell. I turned to prayer and recited scriptures that I had committed to memory. Despite the conditions, I would lift my hands in worship and praise to God. I persisted in this routine until exhaustion overtook me. The concrete floor was too cold to lie upon, and though typically a prisoner in such circumstances would be provided with a flame-retardant mattress, I was denied even this basic comfort. Instead,

I had to squat down, wrap my arms around my knees, and lean against the cold wall in an attempt to rest. Brief periods of sleep would come and go, interrupted by the need to resume pacing once again.

I reached a point where I lost track of whether it was morning or night. Eventually, I heard a metal flap on the cell door open, and a tray slid through it. The tray contained eggs and grits, which in the South is typically served as a breakfast meal, leading me to assume it was between five and eight in the morning. I quickly consumed the food and resumed my pacing and praising routine. This process became my only gauge of time. When a tray was slid through the door, if it contained items like pancakes or eggs, I knew it was morning. If it held rice or beans, I assumed it must be noon or evening. Counting the meal cycles, I realized that I had been enduring this for days.

My friends were left unaware of my whereabouts. I had simply vanished while in the custody of a Mississippi State Trooper. Denied the opportunity to make a phone call, I found solace in the relentless efforts of Chaplain Jim Rentz, who tirelessly sought information on my behalf. Once he learned of my location, he promptly reached out to the chaplain of C.M.C.F. and requested a visit.

One day, a guard opened the cell door and handed me a stiff, padded gown to wear. He informed me that I had a chaplain's visit, though his discomfort was evident. With the officer beside me, I was escorted to a room and seated in front of the chaplain.

The chaplain informed me that Jim Rentz had contacted him out of concern for my well-being and had requested the visit to check on me.

Finally, I felt relieved to have an ally present. With a flood of emotions, I poured out my heart, highlighting the numerous abuses and Constitutional violations I had endured. I made it clear to the chaplain that I was not suicidal and expressed my frustration at not having been allowed a phone call since my arrival at the facility. None of my friends were even aware of my whereabouts.

Desperately, I pleaded for basic necessities such as clothes, a shower, and a toothbrush. The officer, appearing sheepish, glanced at the chaplain and admitted he had not realized I lacked a mattress. Additionally, I questioned why I was being denied access to a Bible.

The chaplain glanced at his watch and determined it was time to conclude our visit. As the guard began to open the door, he leaned in and whispered, "I'll see if I can address your situation with someone, and I'll arrange for a Bible to be sent to you. I'll reassure your friend that you're alright as well." Initially, I entertained the notion that he was discreet in his intentions, but a sudden realization washed over me. This individual was aligned with the institution, or at best, hesitant to confront the injustices within the system. Even more concerning was his intention to assure my friend of my well-being. Internally, I prayed that Chaplain Rentz could discern the true meaning behind this man's words.

The psychiatrist decided to pay me a visit. I couldn't shake the feeling that he derived some sick, morbid satisfaction from observing men pacing back and forth in cells like animals at the zoo. It seemed that, for him, there was a perverse delight in transforming a person into a slobbering zombie simply by administering medication. What a sense of power he must have believed he wielded. This time, I was chained up and brought before him. He began his usual line of questioning, probing into my mental state. I remained composed and reiterated that I harbored no intentions of self-harm. He suggested that I might need to remain on suicide watch a bit longer, emphasizing his concern for my well-being. In response, I stated, "I forgive you for doing this to me. I hold nothing against you." I made it clear that I wouldn't allow this experience to embitter me towards him. His demeanor shifted immediately; disappointment etched across his features.

One day, the officer who opened my tray hatch got distracted and forgot to close and lock it. For the first time, I could see outside my door through the narrow slot and be heard at the same time. Shortly afterward, a female captain entered the area for something. I immediately began calling out to her. She became upset that my tray hatch was left open, but she took a brief second to listen to me. I said, "Captain, Captain, I've been put on suicide watch, but I'm not suicidal! I do not want to be here. I have no intention of hurting myself. Please help me!" Suddenly, she stopped completely and looked sideways at my cell. She asked, "You aren't suicidal?" I replied, "No ma'am." She then inquired, "What are you doing back here?" I explained, "I don't know. I've gone on record to everyone who will listen that I am not suicidal." She turned to an officer in a hallway and said, "If this guy is telling the truth, he has no business back here. To hell with all these egos, we need the room. Lock his tray hatch. I'm going to check on this."

A few hours after our conversation, I was given some clothes, a toothbrush, and toothpaste, and told that I was being transferred to another unit soon. Later, I grabbed a sheet and blanket on my way out. Before I made it off the unit, an officer stopped me and handed me a paperback Bible. He said the chaplain had dropped it off previously. Finally, I could have it. How precious that Bible felt in my hands! It was the strongest weapon I could have in prison.

I entered a processing unit that held each prisoner for a short time while the administration developed multiple files on him: mental health, medical, and classification. Afterwards, each person would be sent to a facility to be housed and finish his sentence. Meanwhile, prisoners were joining gangs for protection or attempting to obtain contraband. This section was a huge dormitory that held hundreds of men. Drug addicts were looking for a fix. Gang members were preying on their weakness. People were being beaten by groups of men all around me for knowingly and unknowingly breaking rules imposed by the gangs. Little did I know, the words of the captain, "we need the room," would make total sense once I saw the chaos and violence that was all around me. Cells were for violent inmates or men who could no longer function in the general population.

I stayed in the processing unit for a couple of months before they decided what to do with me. During this time, I was able to contact my friends through a collect call and let them know I was okay. I kept looking for a miracle, hoping this experience would come to an end. I continued to believe that I would walk out of this place a free man.

One day, I received some mail. Inside the package was all the paperwork I needed to fill out in order to be accepted as faculty at Global University. Despite going through this ordeal, the university's staff still wanted to officially bring me on board.

Deciding to embark on a liquid fast, I pushed aside concerns that I would be too weak to defend myself amidst the violence around me. Instead, I chose to trust in God for the same protection that Daniel received in the Lions' den. Setting aside twenty-one days, I aggressively pursued God in prayer and fasting.

One night, I had the oddest dream. My dear friend and mentor, Jim Rentz, and I were sitting on a bench in a dark subway system, waiting for a train. As the train was pulling up, he told me that I would have to go on without him; he was taking another train. Suddenly, I woke up.

Over the past few weeks, Chaplain Rentz had been trying diligently to help me. He had been in contact with several politicians and M.D.O.C. officials, attempting to secure my release. That same evening I awoke from the dream, I made a telephone call to my other dear friend and mentor, Pastor Carl Everett. I will never forget that call. After greeting each other, Carl said softly, "Alex, Jim Rentz has passed away and gone to be with the Lord." At that moment, I realized that I faced the future on my own. The reality of my previous dream came crashing down on me: Chaplain Rentz was taking another train, and he wouldn't be there to help me.

One day, my brother James sent me a letter asking me to call him. When I did, James informed me that our father's best friend, who also happened to be a distant cousin and a businessman, had been following my situation closely. For years, Jerry Stuart believed that I had been dealt an unfair hand in life, and he felt compelled to act. He believed that God had placed me on his heart.

Mr. Stuart was resolute in his determination to help me. He began reaching out to politicians and leveraging his business connections to advocate for my release. Despite many assurances from these politicians, they failed to deliver on their promises. Mr. Stuart even gathered hundreds of signatures at his business and forwarded them to the governor, hoping for a pardon on my behalf. However, Phil Bryant, upon exiting his office, callously left the community's petition sitting on his desk, refusing to even consider it.

Mr. Stuart grew increasingly disillusioned with the system. Despite years of donating to and supporting candidates in federal, state, and local politics, when he needed their assistance, none of them showed any willingness to help. Nevertheless, in an encouraging gesture, Mr. Stuart sent me a message assuring me that he had secured an apartment and a job for me. All that remained was for a miracle to pave the way for my release.

During my classification interviews, which would determine whether I would be released or start my sentence anew, some peculiar events unfolded. After fasting, I was summoned to the administration building for these crucial interviews. However, they were inexplicably canceled three times in a row. It left me with a strong sense that some sort of spiritual warfare was unfolding over my life.

Finally, I managed to have an interview with a classification officer, but to my dismay, she filled out my paperwork incorrectly. At the time, I was unaware of the error, but she mistakenly classified me as C-custody, which meant Maximum Security. Consequently, I was loaded into a van and transported to Unit 29 at Parchman, famously known as "Castle Grayskull" within the Mississippi State Penitentiary. It was notorious as the place where nightmares were bred in Mississippi.

Upon arrival at Parchman, it became evident to me that certain guards showed deference to specific inmates. It soon dawned on me that these officers weren't the ones truly in charge; it was the gangs that wielded control over the institution.

When I entered the housing unit assigned to me, I encountered an inmate holding a cellphone who promptly initiated a questionnaire. He systematically inquired about my criminal charge, place of origin, gang affiliation, financial status, and interest in various drugs. Essentially, he processed me into the prison akin to the institution's administration. He cross-checked my details against his gang's database to ascertain any outstanding debts, evasion attempts, or potential confidential informant status. A "K.O.S." next to a person's name indicated a directive for "Kill on Sight." After completing his interrogation, he permitted a female officer to escort me to my cell.

This housing unit comprised two levels, with a spacious floor at the bottom. Upstairs cells were granted outdoor time for an hour, while those downstairs remained locked down. Once the upstairs group returned to their cells, it was the turn for the downstairs group to have their recreation time. Despite there being only three payphones available for over a hundred prisoners, the scarcity of payphones was inconsequential as gang members possessed cellphones. They offered significantly lower rates compared to the state for phone usage, charging by the hour. With these illicit phones, individuals could engage in various activities such as accessing social media, checking their Facebook accounts, or Facetiming their partners. Few prioritized working on their legal cases to secure their release from prison. These phones, priced at fifty dollars, fetched six hundred dollars each within the housing unit.

Upon reaching my cell, the officer unlocked the door while my new cellmate was engrossed in a conversation on his cellphone. Stepping inside, I made my way to the available bunk and arranged my belongings. It took a few moments, but we eventually struck up a conversation. He disclosed his affiliation with the Gangster Disciples. Standing at about five feet six inches tall and weighing around a hundred and forty-five pounds, he was twenty-seven years old and serving an eight-year sentence for a shooting incident. I could sense the apprehension in his eyes once he learned about my twenty-five-year stint in Angola. He seemed puzzled about how I had managed to survive for so long. To alleviate his concerns, I shared with him my faith in Jesus, explaining how it had transformed my life. As I spoke, I noticed the tension gradually dissipating from his demeanor.

Over the next several days, he really loosened up. I bought a few food items and shared them with him. He couldn't understand why I was freely offering him something of value with no expectations in return. The following week, he attempted to pay me back. I respectfully declined and explained how God had freely blessed me, so I was being a blessing to him. One evening, he looked at me and confided, "You are an answer to prayer." Intrigued, I asked, "How?" He went on to explain that he was previously locked in this cell with an opposing gang member. He couldn't rest until he knew the other guy was asleep. At any moment, from across the state, for various reasons, the top gang leaders could give a K.O.S. signal by cellphone, igniting a war between the gangs. If he was sleeping, the opposing gang member had the upper hand. He shared that he had prayed for God to place someone in the cell with him who was peaceful and God-fearing.

I wanted to learn more about the gangs. However, when I attempted to ask questions of my cellmate, he threw up his defenses and angrily explained that he was sworn to secrecy. I later learned that if he were to get exposed for having revealed information to me, his life would be in jeopardy. The more I paid attention, the more I saw that the gang members were more fearful of their own gang than the opposing gang. The distrust they had for each other couldn't be hidden from me. If a member broke an established rule of the gang, the ranking members held a court hearing on him. If he was found guilty, he was sanctioned. The term used in prison is "violated." His punishment ranged from two men beating him up for two minutes to being set outside the gang's protection. In other words, he would be on his own for a fixed time, subject to other gangs or whoever wanted to settle a score.

By maintaining silence and observing, I gained insights and adeptly navigated through this corrupt and convoluted world. Astonishingly, I uncovered that some Corrections officers were affiliated with gangs, often hailing from the same neighborhoods as the inmates. Many officers supplemented their modest twenty-four thousand dollar annual salary through illicit contraband sales. Drugs, alcohol, cellphones, and weapons were routinely smuggled into the facility. Female officers were among the prime contributors to this disorder. If not directly affiliated with a gang, they frequently struck deals with them for protection. Gangs would assign a few members to escort these female officers safely around the units, with the officers reciprocating by delivering contraband items in exchange for payment.

Frequently, the female officer assigned to the unit was engaged in a romantic or physical relationship with a gang member. Some of these women had children with prisoners prior to their incarceration, while others deliberately sought employment to be closer to their partners behind bars. Certain individuals initiated relationships with inmates after joining the M.D.O.C. staff. When such a woman entered the workforce, the gang would assume responsibility for her duties. Gang members would handle tasks like delivering mail, completing count sheets, and informing prisoners of appointments for hospital visits or court appearances, among other responsibilities. Meanwhile, she would rendezvous with her partner in a mop closet or another secluded area. It was a frightful thought to realize, "The lunatics were running the insane asylum."

When the meals were delivered, the gangs distributed them without supervision. Each gang took turns in a weekly rotation to maintain peace. This environment witnessed appalling abuses. Adding to the misery, the prison's conditions were so dire that rats would gnaw through bread bags and other food supplies. Even if the gangs managed to distribute the food fairly, some portions were rendered inedible. Roaches and rats plagued the prison, becoming a severe nuisance. Temperatures in the area soared above one hundred degrees Fahrenheit. During attempts to rest at night, wiping sweat from my brow would often reveal a roach crawling across me. It was not uncommon to feel a rat scurry across my bed while lying down. To safeguard food items purchased from the prison commissary, I had to suspend them from the ceiling in bags to deter rats. Despite these intolerable conditions, the gangs refrained from collective complaints. Their involvement in drug use and profiting from contraband sales dissuaded them from drawing attention to the situation.

When gangs administered discipline through beatings, they would conceal the act by hanging up two large sheets, effectively blocking the view of officers. Though officers were aware of the curtain, they purposefully averted their gaze. Non-gang member security officers leveraged the gang structure as a means to maintain order within the prison. They would overlook contraband and gang activity under the tacit understanding that as long as everything remained calm, they would not intervene. However, if fights or violence broke out, security would conduct searches for contraband. Such unwelcome inspections often resulted in the confiscation of valuable items like six-hundred-dollar phones, drugs, and weapons.

A significant amount of illegal activity revolved around phones and the drug trade. I witnessed a scenario where an individual in Maximum Security lockdown orchestrated the delivery of drugs to another prison with the assistance of a corrections officer. The financial transactions among the three parties were facilitated through Cashapp, highlighting the electronic flow of money associated with contraband. This arrangement provided an incentive for high-ranking gang members to minimize violence. However, dealing with volatile and egocentric young men, violence became an unavoidable outcome. When drug addiction further complicated the situation, trouble was virtually guaranteed.

I observed gang members providing drugs to addicts, fully aware that these individuals couldn't afford them. Once the high wore off, gang members would coerce them into paying up. Desperate, the addicts would often call their mothers or grandmothers, pleading for money. While some families could scrape together the funds, many couldn't. When the addict failed to produce the money, they would face brutal beatings by a group of gang members, sometimes resulting in death. To conceal these incidents, the gangs would stage the scene to look like a suicide by hanging the inmate in their cell. They would then report to security that the inmate had taken his own life. In many cases, the security officers either had ties to the gangs or displayed complete apathy, leading to no investigation and no questions asked.

The rules of each gang mandated the provision of a knife to every member. The clip typically utilized for securing an inmate's identification card to his pocket was repurposed with a string to affix each gang member's knife inside his pants, positioned on his hip. Dozens upon dozens of men strolled about, often under the influence and consistently armed. Weapons littered the environment, yet individuals not affiliated with a gang were strictly forbidden from possessing one.

Security officers passed by with an air of indifference. It felt as though we were traversing amidst crates of dynamite, each person carrying a lit match. While members took showers, the gang established a perimeter and stood watch, a practice they referred to as "holding security." Should anyone dare to cross the line, the entire gang would swiftly retaliate.

While I was using the payphone one day, a man was being brutally stabbed and beaten right behind me. My brother, James, heard it over the phone. He exclaimed, "I've got to get you out of there!" After our conversation, he immediately began making calls. He successfully reached out to a local politician in his area, who then made arrangements to have me transferred. The objective was to relocate me to a more manageable facility and utilize my background and education to assist prisoners in obtaining their G.E.D. Shortly thereafter, a classification officer visited my area to verify my transfer request.

He informed me that I had to pay the state in order to be transferred to another facility. If I signed the paperwork, the state would deduct the money from my account. I speculated that this visit was a result of my brother's phone calls. I inquired, "Where am I being transferred?" He replied, "Marshall County Correctional Facility (M.C.C.F.)…Maximum Security. That's the only place we can send you because of your custody status." I realized I wasn't being transferred to a more manageable facility. Instead, I was about to pay to be shipped to another lions' den.

This facility had recently made headlines on televised news. An officer had been beaten unconscious, and the housing unit was set on fire. The perpetrators, gang members, filmed the incident with their phones, and someone posted the video on social media. Upon my arrival, I underwent swift processing and was escorted to the Maximum-Security unit that had garnered media attention. After assigning me a cell, the young officer opened the heavy door and in a somber tone, said, "Good luck." As I stepped into the unit, the massive door slammed shut behind me. I attempted to walk to my assigned cell, but a gang member suddenly rose from a table to my left and began yelling, "Hey y'all, I don't want him in my cell....Ya heard. I don't want him in my cell!"

Suddenly, about seven armed gang members stood together in a line in front of the cell. The apparent leader said, "You can't live here." In their gang hierarchy, if a member objected to someone assigned by security sharing their cell, the gang was obliged to unite and demand a transfer, often through violent means. Security had effectively ceded control of the living area to the gangs, allowing them to dictate where inmates slept or even if they remained on the unit. Unaware of these dynamics, I attempted to gather information by asking one of them a question. However, my ignorance of their self-imposed rules was interpreted as resistance. With knives drawn, they began to hype themselves up for an attack. By the grace of God, I swiftly turned around and began walking away.

The leader of the opposing gang was awakened and informed that there might be trouble brewing on his unit. Concerned about potential disruptions to his illicit operations by officers, he summoned me to his area. After interrogating me, he granted permission for me to reside upstairs in the area under his control. His exact words were, "He can bunk with Crazy man." Though not exactly reassuring, these words marked a beginning. As a fellow inmate helped me lug my mattress, he remarked, "Bro, this guys is throw'd off. You gotta be something serious to live with him." Upon swinging open the cell door, the pungent odor hit me like a wave. It was the height of summer, and the occupant of my new living quarters hadn't taken a shower in months.

This man's hair and fingernails had grown excessively long from lack of grooming. He remained confined within his cell, rarely venturing outside. His routine consisted of lying on a plastic mattress drenched in sweat throughout the day and into the night. Upon the arrival of each meal tray, he would rise to consume it using his bare hands. Following his meal, he would regurgitate into the sink and agitate the contents with his fingers until they disappeared down the drain. This unsettling ritual recurred in the dead of night; I would awaken to find him conversing with himself while repeating the nauseating process of swirling vomit in the sink. The overpowering stench compelled me to tie a t-shirt around my face just to endure the odor and find sleep.

The cell doors remained open at all times, despite being in Maximum Security. Most of the lights had been vandalized; gangs tore out electrical wires to power their cellphone chargers. To escape the suffocating darkness and stench akin to a decaying animal, I often ventured outside the cell to read. It felt like inhabiting a cavern with a lingering, foul presence. Despite the conditions, my commitment to reading drew some attention. As I consistently turned down drugs and treated others with respect, inmates began to engage in conversation with me. This provided an opportunity to share my faith and talk about Jesus.

One particularly imposing figure, known as a formidable enforcer for his gang, was captivated by my account of Angola's transformation. He found the miracles I spoke of intriguing, sparking his own curiosity about whether the Mississippi system could undergo similar change.

Eventually, I managed to obtain the paperwork from M.D.O.C. revealing that the classification officer had erroneously placed me in C-custody, designated for Maximum Security. I sent it via mail to a lawyer who assured me he would contact the head of classification in an attempt to rectify the situation. Meanwhile, as I awaited a resolution, I was struck with the excruciating pain of a kidney stone.

The medical emergency was utterly dreadful. The combination of nausea and excruciating pain left me on the brink of passing out. Desperate for assistance, I reached out to the security personnel. However, the officer I pleaded with treated me with utter disdain. I collapsed to the ground, clutching onto a nearby chair like a child seeking comfort from their mother. Despite my distress, he callously demanded that I return to the chair and sit properly. He continued to berate me and even went so far as to inspect my fingers for burn marks, suspecting drug use. In between agonizing moans, I managed to protest, "I wasn't using drugs. Something is seriously wrong with me!" At that moment, I was utterly clueless about the nature of my affliction.

Finally, a nurse arrived and felt a little sympathy towards me, helping me up to take a urine screen. Upon reviewing the results, they discovered blood in my urine. The officer remained convinced of my involvement in illegal activity, demanding, "Who did you get into a fight with?" Exhausted, I could no longer contend with him. He seemed to drone on like the adults in a Charlie Brown cartoon. Then, I vomited. That was enough to make him leave. I was rushed to a hospital in a nearby town and treated for a kidney stone. The doctor informed me that surgery was necessary due to the damage inflicted by the stone on my kidney walls.

I signed the necessary paperwork and returned to the prison. However, when it was time for the surgery, I learned that the warden had canceled the hospital trip, unwilling to bear the cost of the surgery. Once again, I found myself in a helpless situation. I prayed fervently, "Lord, this could seriously harm me. I need your intervention. Please heal me or find a way to get me to the hospital." Shortly thereafter, an officer came to my unit and instructed me to gather my belongings and follow him. I was being transferred to the general population.

When I arrived at the new unit, I underwent the familiar interview process with the gangs. They brought out their cellphones, and we went through their questions. However, this time, these guys couldn't quite grasp what I was saying. One of them looked at me and remarked, "You don't look like a prisoner. You don't sound like a prisoner." Another one added, "You don't have any tattoos." Another guy piped up, "Maybe he's F.B.I.?" Eventually, another guy chimed in, "No, no, I know who this guy is. He's a reality star. Man, this dude is trying to see if he can survive 60 days on the inside. We're on TV right now. They're watching us!"

By this time, all the gangs had gathered around me to see what the commotion was about. Our previous interaction had drawn a crowd.

Now, I found myself surrounded by the Simon City Royals, the Bloods, the Gangster Disciples, the Aryan Brotherhood, the Latin Kings, the Vice Lords, and the Crips. Unsure of what else to do, I did the only thing I knew: I preached about Jesus. I shared how the Lord had completely transformed my life and rescued me from Angola. Gradually, the crowd began to disperse, and eventually, everyone left me alone. Afterwards, each group observed me closely. Soon enough, they realized that I was indeed what I claimed to be.

Gang members would discreetly approach me, seeking prayer. They confided in me that they desired the transformation they witnessed in me, but were unable to leave their respective groups due to the severe consequences they would face. Essentially, these individuals were trapped by fear. It was clear that attempting to break away from their gangs could potentially cost them their lives. Within the prison system, there was no refuge from the pervasive influence of the gangs. Due to the widespread use of cellphones and the extensive network of the gangs, even if they managed to transfer to another facility, the gang would have its members waiting for them upon their arrival.

This is how a basic gang structure operated within the Mississippi system. For instance, in a prison with five units, each unit consisted of four housing areas. Each housing area was overseen by a "house man" who exerted control and took responsibility for his gang members within that area. Supporting him was a lieutenant, serving as his second-in-command. Below them were foot soldiers, each with their own ranks and duties. One lower-ranking member might be tasked with monitoring rival gang movements and gathering intelligence, while another might be responsible for conducting interviews with new prisoners. Reports from various positions were expected to be submitted to the house man by the end of each day.

Once the house man received the day's briefings, he convened a Zoom call with the other house men from the housing areas within his unit. The unit's overseer then facilitated a meeting with all the house men in the unit. Subsequently, each unit leader participated in another Zoom call with the individual in charge of the entire prison. These leaders, in turn, connected via Zoom with the overseer of the entire state. This interconnected network spanned the entire prison system. With the simple push of a button on a cellphone, a gang war could erupt from one end of the state to the other, as indeed occurred.

I went to bed one night and opened my eyes to what could only be described as a living nightmare. The entire system of gangs had gone to war with each other. The mayhem that ensued resembled the movie, Mad Max Beyond Thunder dome. The two most powerful groups who opposed each other had divided the housing units in the aftermath. All the men who were not affiliated with gangs now had to sleep in the middle of the unit and act as a buffer zone between the warring groups. Dozens and dozens of men were killed. Fires had been started on certain prison units. Electric power to many of those units had been turned off, so a lot of this chaos continued in the dark. Finally, the National Guard and State Police were called to stop the riot and restore order.

The administrative officials at the helm of M.D.O.C. resigned from their positions amid disgrace. In response, Governor Tate Reeves swiftly embarked on a quest to find a new Commissioner to lead the Department of Corrections. Providentially, Warden Burl Cain emerged from retirement and applied for the position. Following discussions with the governor, Reeves appointed Cain to the role, a decision subsequently ratified by the legislature. Commissioner Cain wasted no time in initiating reforms to revitalize the system.

Since Cain had been informed of my situation prior to becoming Commissioner, after his appointment, he made a call to the prison that held me and told the warden to give me a Bible and turn me loose to preach. Until then, the entire M.D.O.C would not allow an inmate to teach, preach, or start a church. The idea that was promulgated was that no inmate would have authority over another inmate. This reasoning evolved as a result of state governments in the South during the 1960s and 1970s getting rid of armed inmate guards to oversee fellow inmates. The modern-day interpretation of this rule did not allow inmates to participate in positive prosocial change inside the system.

Over the years, the policy has continued to evolve and be applied to church participation in prison. This penological mindset has prevented inmates from leading in formal Bible studies and worship services. Consequently, this practice has led to a positive leadership vacuum among inmates. Men naturally tend to follow other men, and when positive models are prohibited, gangs quickly step in to fill the void. This issue is exacerbated when institutions fail to adequately protect inmates from violence. The church plays a crucial role in offering acceptance, significance, and safety to inmates. When the inmate church is not permitted to provide these essential elements, gangs inevitably take over, offering a harmful and counterfeit substitute. Essentially, the policy only hinders the efforts of the "good guys" (the church), while gangs operate with little regard for rules, akin to gangsters ignoring gun laws in Chicago.

When Cain reached out, I was granted the opportunity to preach five services in a single day. Cain, in his satisfaction, contacted the governor and proudly exclaimed, "We're transforming the prison system. Today, I made my first inmate pastor." Governor Reeves was so impressed by the news that he shared it on his Facebook page. As word spread throughout the prison, more and more inmates expressed a desire to attend church. However, the classroom initially allocated to us couldn't accommodate everyone. Within a few weeks, we obtained permission to use the gym for weekend services. At our inaugural service, we filled the space to its capacity.

While I was ministering in the M.D.O.C., Mr. Stuart voiced his concerns about my situation to a visiting judge at his business one day. After hearing him out, the judge uttered words that would alter the course of my life: "Tell Alex to send me a motion, and I'll let him out." It was as straightforward as that. Immediately, Mr. Jerry consulted a lawyer about filing the motion. I can only imagine the greedy grin on the lawyer's face when she informed my father's friend that she required thirty thousand dollars to file a single piece of paper with the courts. Upon learning this, I adamantly refused to allow anyone to pay such an exorbitant sum for what seemed like a simple task. I couldn't bring myself to agree to it. Instead, I took it upon myself to research the law and draft the motion. Armed with four sheets of typing paper and an ink pen, I meticulously crafted the document. I affixed two stamps to the envelope and mailed it to the Clerk of Court. The motion was filed, and it promptly made its way to the judge, who granted it and forwarded it to the Parole Board, ordering my immediate release.

Instead of an immediate release, the board somehow misplaced the order that was sent to them from the judge. Consequently, I remained incarcerated for another five months. Throughout this period, I remained faithful and continued to serve God with my whole heart, unaware of what had occurred. However, I couldn't shake the feeling that something was amiss. After the fifth month, I requested Crystal to reach out to the friendly lawyer who had assisted me in getting released from Maximum Security. Upon his intervention, he promptly contacted the head of the parole board. Diplomatically, he explained that the judge had granted my motion and ordered my immediate release. In response, the Chairman assured, "No problem. We'll locate that paperwork and have him processed today."

Chapter 8

Delivered

fter twenty-six years, on October 26, 2020, I was on the cusp of stepping into the free world. Crystal arrived to pick me up, but the prison informed us that their warehouse was closed, preventing them from providing me with clothes to leave the facility. We would have to wait until the following day for access. Crystal, in a panic, declared, "I will go and buy him some clothes." She had taken time off work and driven nearly three hundred miles to pick me up. Though not a fan of Walmart, I thanked God that they were open that day. She hurriedly purchased a pair of black stretch pants (the kind that would get a guy into serious trouble in prison) and a gray thermal shirt. Upon her return to the prison, she handed the clothes over to the officials, who promptly delivered them to me. Clark Kent, Superman's alter ego, couldn't have changed clothes any faster than I did. In a flash, I swapped outfits and headed for the door.

Normally, a guy leaving prison would be provided with his identification and any money he had in his account. Angola had released me to Mississippi with all the necessary identification to kickstart my life. However, an officer somewhere in M.D.O.C. made the decision to discard my State I.D., Social Security Card, Birth Certificate, and Insurance Card. Furthermore, only half of the money I had saved for years was deposited in Western Union for me to claim, while the other half was issued to me in a check. It soon dawned on me that I couldn't cash the check or claim the money from Western Union without proper identification. In fact, I realized that I couldn't reintegrate into society without identification at all. Thankfully, several months prior to my release, a friend had gifted me a few hundred dollars. I suggested to Crystal that she keep it for cash on hand and use it to purchase a phone for me. Additionally, I thought it would be fitting to take her out to a restaurant for our first meal together in the free world.

Prior to my release, I was informed that I had to report to my Mississippi parole officer within twenty-four hours, or I would risk being violated and sent back to prison. Ironically, Louisiana had also instructed me to report to my parole officer there within forty-eight hours prior to my release, under the same consequence of being sent back to prison if I failed to comply. Essentially, I was expected to be in two states at once while serving parole. While this situation had the potential to cause me significant stress, I had learned that God doesn't split the Red Sea to leave you in the Wilderness. We can trust Him to carry us through difficulties.

When the last prison gate opened, Crystal stood waiting for me. Stepping across the threshold into freedom after more than a quarter of a century of incarceration, it didn't seem real. I felt a wave of concern, half expecting to wake from an incredible dream. Crystal wrapped her arms around me, welcoming me to freedom with a kiss. We hurried to her car, as if fearing they might change their minds and call me back.

As we left the parking lot, she handed me a box containing a cell phone. Crystal assumed everyone knew how to turn on and operate a cell phone, but I had never used one before today. I definitely needed her help. Pulling into a Western Union parking lot, we activated my phone together. I felt like Captain Kirk of the U.S. Enterprise.

Previously, as I made my way out of the prison, I discreetly raised the issue of my missing identification. The attendant at the front desk of M.C.C.F. printed out a picture of me along with my prison details. "Maybe this will help you," she offered. I couldn't help but notice that the document in my hand looked like something a ten-year-old could have produced using basic word processing software.

Unfortunately, my attempt to use the printout to claim my money at Western Union was futile. I couldn't blame the employee for rejecting it;

after all, I was trying to claim thousands of dollars with a mere Xerox copy of my prison ID. The situation left me feeling a mix of embarrassment and frustration. Nonetheless, despite the unpleasantness of the incident, I was now free. I reassured myself that this problem would eventually be resolved.

Leaving Western Union, we got into the car and drove towards freedom, I shared with Crystal that the first person I wanted to text was Dr. Randy Hedlun from Global University.

I texted Dr. Hedlun with these words, "Hey Dr. Hedlun, just escaped. Headed to Mexico. All prayers are welcome!" To my surprise, when he received the text, he genuinely believed it to be true. He immediately called his wife over and exclaimed, "Jacie, Alex has finally broken. He's escaped. Let's pray for God to have mercy." Together, this dear couple began fervently praying for my safety. If the situation weren't so amusing, I might have felt guilty.

Eventually, Dr. Hedlun had the thought to text me and confirm whether I was serious. I quickly reassured him that everything was alright. I was legally free, and with God's grace, I would soon see him. Meanwhile, as Crystal and I chuckled and drove down the road, my phone rang for the first time. I answered it cautiously, saying, "Hello?" On the other end of the line was Mrs. Ruth Graham. Unless God had supernaturally distributed my number to His faithful servants, I assumed Dr. Hedlun had provided it to her. Mrs. Graham expressed her excitement for me and extended her wishes for a brighter future ahead.

Crystal and I decided to make a pit stop at Walmart to grab some snacks for the road trip. While Crystal browsed for items, I headed to the bathroom. Upon entering, I couldn't help but notice the absence of handles on the sinks. It struck me that things had certainly changed since my time of incarceration when sinks still had handles.

"Wow. I can figure this one out," I mused to myself as I attempted to activate the sink by waving my hand in front of it. However, as fate would have it, the motion detectors on at least two out of five sinks at Walmart rarely seemed to work. I hadn't known that at the time.

Pondering my next move, I entertained the thought, "Maybe it's voice-activated." After all, according to tradition, Moses was supposed to speak to the rock for water to flow. I couldn't help but chuckle inwardly at the absurdity of the situation, hoping no one would walk in while I was having my moment of confusion.

After some trial and error, I decided to try the sink next to me by waving my hand. To my relief, water started pouring out of the faucet. Later, when recounting the ordeal to Crystal, I joked that I felt like Moses trying to command the water from that sink.

Crystal and I embarked on a non-stop drive from Marshall County to Lamar County, where I needed to report to my parole officer. With the prevailing fears surrounding the pandemic, tension hung heavy in the air. Understandably cautious, my female parole officer preferred I remain outside the building while she conducted our meeting through a crack in the door.

Through some persuasive negotiation, I managed to obtain a pass allowing me to travel to Louisiana to address my situation and facilitate a transfer back to Mississippi. Crystal, true to her word, assured me she would accompany me on the journey.

The following day, I found myself once again seated beside Crystal as she navigated us towards Baton Rouge, Louisiana. The bustling lights, vibrant colors, and fast-paced traffic overwhelmed my senses, yet amidst it all, we found solace in conversation and laughter, weaving our way through the trip together.

Once I arrived, the Louisiana parole department initially didn't believe a word I told them. Their skepticism was palpable. One person insisted I was overdue to report to them by a year. There were even threats of violating me. After phone calls and record checks, some of the staff finally changed their tone and began working toward a remedy. They decided to charge me over two hundred dollars to enact the Interstate Compact agreement and transfer me to Mississippi. If I didn't pay the bill, I would go back to prison. Thank goodness, I had instructed Crystal to hold some of my money. In the meantime, they issued me a work pass for three months to return to Mississippi. They assumed this would provide enough time for the transfer to take place. Otherwise, I couldn't stay in Mississippi. Essentially, through no fault of my own, I was dangerously close to getting violated and sent back to prison by laws and policies that were unable to take into account my situation. Lady Justice is truly blindfolded.

Crystal and I loaded ourselves into the car and headed back to Mississippi. Along the way, we stopped at a bank and tried to cash my check. The bank teller kindly informed me that I would at least need a

State ID. Shortly after arriving in the Magnolia State, I went to work for Mr. Stuart. He owned a Hardware and Feed store with an apartment above it and a Fertilizer Company. I started at the bottom of his business and began working hard. However, I quickly ran into a problem. My work responsibilities demanded that I drive, but my driver's license had expired two decades ago. I needed to get it renewed. If I could obtain a State ID, I could solve a lot of problems and access my money from that check and Western Union. Mr. Stuart tossed me his keys and instructed me to take his truck to get my driver's license renewed.

I wish I could tell you that I didn't drive myself there without a license, but Crystal was at work, and everyone else I knew was occupied as well. Since the pandemic struck, no one was allowed into the Department of Motor Vehicles to stand in line. The sign on the door said, "Go online and set up an appointment." The problem was that I had never done anything like this online. Fortunately, a lady was standing beside me, so I asked her to help me. Without batting an eye, she took my phone and set up an appointment for me.

Once inside, I talked to an employee and told him that my Driver's license expired over two decades ago and that I would like to get it renewed. Unfortunately, no records existed in the Department of Transportation's computers concerning me. The man talking to me said that I would have to apply for a Driver's license all over again similar to when I was a teenager. That process included taking the written test again. I asked what I needed to start the process. He said that I needed a Social Security Card. I decided to go to the Social Security office and apply for a card. Again, I had to go online and interact with someone. This person told me that I needed a State I.D. to secure a Social Security Card. In other words, I needed a Social Security card to get a State I.D., but I needed a State I.D. to get a Social Security Card. Either way, I ran into a dead end.

After spending days on the phone and communicating online, I decided to try locating my immunization records with the Health Department. I walked into the Health Department in Purvis, Mississippi, and asked for my immunization records. The lady went into the back, dusted off a file, and handed me a copy of the records. I also managed to secure my birth certificate online. Next, I packaged both records in an envelope and sent them to the Social Security Office. Within a couple of weeks, my Social Security Card arrived in the mail. This little piece of paper allowed me to join the rest of society and access my money.

Within a few months, Mr. Stuart entrusted me with keys to everything, including his buildings, vehicles, cash registers, and safe, demonstrating a profound level of trust. However, he was aware of my deep-seated commitment to serving the Lord. He assured me that whenever I felt the need to prioritize my religious duties, I was free to do so. Soon after, Global University began assigning distance students to me. I took charge of overseeing their coursework and grading their papers online. Additionally, discussions within Global's leadership emerged regarding the possibility of relocating me to Springfield, Mo.

Upon learning of my availability, Scott Holmes extended an invitation for me to accompany him on a tour through eleven churches in Louisiana. Filled with excitement, I promptly sought permission from my parole officer to embark on this journey. I believed this opportunity could potentially be transformative for my ministry and career, especially considering that several of the churches were in need of a full-time pastor. Additionally, I anticipated that my parole officer would view this as a positive outlet for me to utilize my education and experience. However, to my disappointment, she denied my request to travel. Both she and her supervisor objected to the idea of me engaging in any church-related activities.

Shocked by the denial, I made a conscious effort to readjust my attitude and persevered in working six days a week for Mr. Stuart. Internally, I grappled with conflicting emotions regarding my sense of calling and the seemingly insurmountable obstacle before me. I had always envisioned stepping directly into ministry upon my release from prison, and my current circumstances felt bewildering. For more than half of my life, I had been certain of God's call for me to spread His word to the nations, yet I encountered closed doors at every turn.

Then, a glimmer of hope emerged when I received an invitation to visit the Church of the Highlands in Birmingham, Alabama. Longtime friends, who had graciously welcomed me into their home after my conversion, had relocated to support Chris Hodges' vision for establishing a church in Birmingham. Both had risen to prominence within the congregation and were extending an invitation for me to witness the remarkable growth of this ministry firsthand. Filled with anticipation, I saw this trip as a potential pathway to discovering a place to serve alongside them.

Unfortunately, upon submitting the Church's formal invitation and my request to travel to my parole officer, she and her supervisor responded with a firm "No." Once again, the door was closed to me. My heartfelt desire to serve in ministry seemed thwarted by the opposition from those in authority over me.

However, one day while contemplating my predicament, the phone rang. It was Dr. Randy Hedlun, reaching out to brief me on a development within the Board of Administrators (B.O.A.) at the university. They were considering bringing me in for an interview. The prospect of working full-time for this World Missions-minded school filled me with excitement, and I wasted no time in preparing for the interview.

Eventually, the date for the interview was set, and I appeared before the B.O.A. via Zoom. The meeting unfolded differently than I had anticipated. Throughout our time together, I received only one question from a member until Dr. Hedlun broke the silence with another inquiry. By then, the quiet had become so pronounced that it felt deafening. I stumbled through my initial response, akin to a freshman quarterback fumbling the ball during his debut play. When Dr. Hedlun posed another question, I couldn't help but wonder if he was attempting to offer me another chance to redeem myself, like a coach calling for a second attempt at a successful play.

As the interview drew to a close, I found myself wanting to retreat and hide. However, Dr. Hedlun and Dr. Seevers, the president, reassured me that they would inform me of the B.O.A.'s decision in due course. To shield myself emotionally, I resigned to considering it a loss in my mind and resolved to continue pushing forward. I had given it my best effort. What more could I ask of myself?

A few days later, while I was working under the Mississippi sun, my cellphone rang. It was Dr. Seevers. He asked if I had a moment to talk, and I assured him that I did. He then extended the official invitation: an offer to join Springfield, MO and Global University as a full-time faculty member at their headquarters. Along with the invitation, he outlined the benefits package and offered a salary. Without hesitation, I accepted the offer. There was no need for a burning bush or an angelic apparition to confirm this decision; I had spent half my life preparing for this opportunity.

Filled with joy, I rushed to the parole office to share the good news. I requested a transfer to Missouri to begin my new career. Although the parole officer seemed reluctant, she took down my information and submitted the transfer request.

She confessed to me that she struggled to grasp the requirements and procedures she needed to follow. Essentially, she couldn't fully comprehend the policies governing my situation. To her credit, she sought assistance, but unfortunately, her supervisor appeared equally uncertain. My parole officer assembled a transfer request and sent it to Missouri via email. I returned to work and awaited a response. A few weeks later, she phoned to inform me that Missouri had rejected the request, citing dissatisfaction with the paperwork. She assured me she would make another attempt.

This back-and-forth between Missouri and Mississippi persisted for over a year. During this period, Commissioner Cain learned that my parole officer was hindering my ability to travel and minister. He seized this situation as an opportunity to address the heads of the Parole department and reform their culture and approach. Essentially, his philosophical solution was straightforward: "You will not prevent them from attending church; you need to facilitate their attendance." The underlying aim was to encourage pro-social activities. While I cannot claim that the entire state immediately embraced his vision, this redirection was sufficient to eventually grant me the freedom to travel and minister.

The university sought to facilitate the transfer process, so they contacted the Missouri Parole department to inquire about the status of my case. State officials informed them that the way Mississippi was submitting the paperwork rendered it unacceptable under the law for Missouri to proceed. Consequently, Missouri reached out to the Mississippi Parole department and provided guidance on how to properly complete the paperwork to expedite the process.

However, when my parole officer finally completed the transfer paperwork correctly, she mistakenly listed the wrong address where I would be staying. As a result, my request was once again rejected. After rectifying this error and ensuring the correct address was included, my paperwork was finally set in motion.

When Missouri received the documents, a parole officer was

assigned to verify the address where I would be residing. Dr. Clinton Caszatt, a retired military Colonel, former Missouri Department of Corrections chaplain, professor at Global University, and Chairman of my dissertation committee, graciously offered to open his home to me until I could secure a place of my own. Following discussions with Dr. Caszatt, the parole officer opted to deny the transfer, citing my lack of family ties in Missouri.

Since Dr. Caszatt also held a position at the university, the parole officer expressed concerns about the potential risks involved in allowing me to relocate. He argued that if my employment situation were to falter, so too could my housing stability. The parole officer expressed doubts about entrusting my wellbeing and adherence to prosocial behavior to a Christian professor and a Christian university. In his documented opinion, he believed that my transfer could potentially lead to a recurrence of criminal behavior, resulting in a return to prison. Consequently, he deemed the transfer too hazardous for me to proceed with.

Following the denial from Missouri, Dr. Caszatt, along with two other professors, participated in a seminar in Dallas, Texas, hosted by Commissioner Burl Cain. Commissioner Cain aimed to foster collaboration between Christian colleges and Departments of Correction nationwide through the establishment of a new organization called the Prison Seminaries Foundation. His vision was to facilitate the development of a relationship between these entities, ultimately leading to the implementation of seminaries within the prison system, akin to the successful model at Angola.

During breaks between sessions, Dr. Caszatt took the opportunity to speak with Commissioner Cain, expressing his frustration: "We've been trying to facilitate Alex's transfer to Missouri for over a year now. We have a job available on staff with full benefits. The refusal to allow him to move seems illogical. In fact, we wanted him here with us. However, the parole board has consistently denied his requests to travel for speaking engagements or ministry opportunities. Is there anything you can do?" Cain promptly replied, "I can arrange his transfer if that's what you want."

As Cain directed his team to investigate my transfer, he convened key individuals in the legislature, as well as judges and district attorneys. Leveraging my haphazard release from M.D.O.C., he spearheaded the creation of new legislation. Henceforth, no inmate would depart a Mississippi prison without their identification and essential documentation. It became mandatory by law for M.D.O.C. to provide discharging inmates with all necessary identification. Cain cited my experience as a catalyst for improving the system, ensuring better outcomes for those who would follow in my footsteps.

One day, I inquired with my parole officer about the remaining duration of my parole. She informed me that my Mississippi parole was nearing its end, but due to my Louisiana sentence, I would have to remain on parole for another 12 years. I found it difficult to believe her interpretation of the situation. Taking matters into my own hands, I contacted Commissioner Cain and explained the situation. Upon his directive, his team delved into my case. Following their investigation, their computer system at the state capital indicated an immediate release for me. Cain personally reached out to me and delivered the news: I was no longer bound by parole. With his words, "Alex Hennis, you are a free man. You are completely free to go preach the gospel. Now, go do what Jesus told you to do," it felt as though a thousand pounds had been lifted from my shoulders.

He instructed me to wait a couple of weeks before departing until I received the discharge paperwork from M.D.O.C. I phoned Crystal and shared the good news with her. However, she quickly became apprehensive that I might leave for Missouri immediately and leave her behind. I had no intention of dishonoring all those years she had patiently waited for me. Therefore, I purchased a ring and discreetly visited her workplace before her shift ended.

I had planned a romantic proposal, intending to kneel with the wedding ring as she entered her workplace. As she opened the door, there I was, on one knee with the ring held up. However, her response was unexpected. She sharply exclaimed, "Get up from there before you embarrass me!" My attempt at romance fell flat.

Later, when we were alone, I shared my heartfelt intentions with her. I expressed my desire to dedicate the rest of my life to the gospel, investing my gifts, talents, and resources into furthering God's kingdom. I offered her the opportunity to join her life with mine in marriage.

A friend later remarked, "Alex, that's not a marriage proposal. That's an altar call."

Chapter 9

To the Ends of the Earth

T

he release papers from M.D.O.C. with its gold seal finally arrived, marking my official freedom. Crystal and I wasted no time and tied the knot the very next day.

The morning after our wedding, I hastily packed all my belongings into my car, including a coffee pot, and embarked on a nine and a half-hour journey to Springfield, Missouri. With Dr. Cazatte away on a ministry trip, Dr. Hedlun graciously opened his home to me upon my arrival.

The following day, Dr. Hedlun kindly drove me to work, where I started my new job at Global University under the name Dr. Alex Hennis. With Crystal in mind, one of my top priorities was to swiftly secure a place we could call home in Missouri.

Upon applying for a loan, I encountered an unexpected hurdle. It turned out that during my hospitalization while in the Mississippi prison, the bill for my medical care had been reported as an outstanding debt on my credit report. This revelation was disheartening, compounded by the fact that I essentially didn't exist for the two and a half decades in the eyes of financial institutions. Consequently, I shifted my focus to securing a rental house while I worked on building up an acceptable credit score.

Upon my arrival in Springfield, the President of Global University, Dr. Gary Seevers, approached me and asked if I would be interested in speaking at the Ritz-Carlton in Georgia to a gathering of pastors from across the country. These remarkable men had cultivated thriving churches that had deeply impacted numerous lives, and they played a crucial role in supporting Global's mission to reach out to the lost and empower the faithful. Now, I found myself honored to stand before them and offer insight into their journey. Following the sharing of some aspects of my personal testimony, several pastors approached me, expressing interest in staying connected. They eagerly requested my contact information, expressing their desire to have me minister in their

142

respective churches.

Upon my return to Springfield, I received an invitation from Doug Lowenberg, who was overseeing Addis Ababa Bible College in Ethiopia. He extended a formal invitation for me to teach a Greek Romans exegetical course to his Master's students. Without any hesitation, I readily accepted his invitation. Despite not knowing how I would finance the trip to Addis Ababa, Ethiopia, I was fully committed to going anywhere on the planet to advance the gospel of Jesus Christ. I trusted that God would pave the way.

As I geared up for the upcoming class, I received an email from Pastor Rob Ketterling's associate pastor, Dave Phillips. In the email, he formally extended an invitation for me to visit Minneapolis, Minnesota, to minister downtown, particularly in the areas affected by the events surrounding the George Floyd case. They arranged to fly me to Minneapolis and then drive me to various ministry locations. Without hesitation, I accepted the invitation. Upon my arrival, I delivered a sermon at a newly established downtown campus. Additionally, Pastor Ketterling gathered his leadership team from across the state, providing me with the opportunity to address them. Later on, I had the privilege of visiting and preaching in some halfway houses overseen by Pastor Phillips.

These halfway houses served as residences for men either sentenced by a judge or voluntarily seeking assistance based on their individual needs. Staff members at these homes worked diligently to help residents secure employment, improve social skills, and attend substance abuse classes. It was a privilege for me to teach a diverse group of individuals, including convicted felons, drug addicts, and men awaiting trial for their offenses.

A rough looking, motorcycle gang leader was present. He had committed another crime while he was on parole. He was in the Half-way house awaiting trial. This guy still held a tremendous amount of influence in Minnesota's prison system because of his position in the gang. Prison is all he knew. He spent most of his adult life going in and out of the system. He listened intently to what I was saying. When I gave the altar call to receive Jesus and be filled with the Holy Spirit, he came forward with tears in his eyes. In obedience to God's word, I laid my hands on him, and he was filled with the Holy Spirit and began speaking in other tongues (Acts 8:17).

After concluding the ministry opportunities, I was chauffeured to the airport, where I was handed an envelope containing a check. I quickly tucked it into my laptop bag, exchanged farewells with handshakes and hugs, and proceeded to find my departing flight. Upon arriving home and beginning to unpack my belongings, I suddenly recollected the envelope containing the check stowed away in my laptop bag. Retrieving it, I opened the envelope, and to my astonishment, a check slipped out, bearing an amount sufficient to cover all the expenses for the trip to Ethiopia that I had agreed to earlier. It was undeniable evidence of God's provision, making a way where I saw none.

Upon returning to my office, I was surprised to find an email from my ex-parole officer in Mississippi, urgently requesting that I call her without delay. Naively, I hoped that perhaps she wanted to hear about the positive developments in my life. However, when I dialed her number and she picked up, I was taken aback by her revelation. She informed me that there had been an error in my case. Despite Commissioner Cain's pronouncement of my freedom, it was apparently a mistake, and I was required to return to Mississippi immediately. Stunned and disbelieving, I insisted on speaking to her supervisor to seek clarification on the matter.

Gratefully, my ex-parole officer provided me with her supervisor's contact information, and I wasted no time in placing the call. To my dismay, the supervisor was forthcoming and explained that she had unearthed an error stemming from Commissioner Cain's oversight. Apparently, the computers used by his staff lacked the pertinent information regarding my Louisiana case. Despite the discharge of my Mississippi case, Louisiana authorities still expected Mississippi to retain me on parole for another ten years. Shockingly, it dawned on me that I was currently residing in Missouri unlawfully. The supervisor issued a stern ultimatum: unless I returned to Mississippi immediately, I would face arrest.

I said, "Ma'am, I have a ministry and career here. This is where I live. This is where I work now. I have nowhere to live in Mississippi. Where do you want me to live? Under a bridge?" I will never forget her words or tone, "I don't care where you live. All I care about is you getting here… Now! You need to check in with us and report… Immediately!" In disbelief, I just held the phone to my ear. Eventually, she must have hung up. I started calling people to see if they would help me.

I called Mrs. Graham and Mrs. Brandes. They both, in turn, called Commissioner Cain. Cain contacted his connections in the Louisiana government who later reached out to me. Mississippi and Louisiana aligned their stance and agreed not to pursue my arrest for leaving the state of Mississippi. A very astute but blunt individual in Louisiana opted to implement the Interstate Compact agreement, transferring my parole oversight to Missouri. This action would prevent me from facing jail time, but it meant that I was now under the jurisdiction of the State of Missouri.

After several days, I was assigned a new Missouri D.O.C. number and instructed to report immediately to my new parole officer. I left the university and promptly reported to my new overseer. To my surprise, he turned out to be the same individual who had denied my parole transfer from Mississippi to Dr. Caszatt's house. He had expressed concerns that my relocation might lead to reoffending and a return to prison. Ironically, I would have to develop a relationship with the guy who didn't want me here in the first place.

After we met, I paid strict attention to the rules he set up. He expected me to report to him regularly and be ready for surprise inspections at my house and work. I watched his face carefully as I explained that I was a professor who was expected to travel internationally. I also brought him the necessary paperwork concerning the class I would be teaching in Ethiopia. Surprisingly, he told me that if I was traveling internationally, I didn't need a pass from him. However, if I was traveling in the United States, I had to have a pass to cross state lines. In other words, I could fly anywhere in the world outside the United States, but if I drove a car across the Missouri state line, I needed a pass from him.

Soon, I found myself on a plane headed to Addis Ababa, Ethiopia. Upon arrival in the capital city, I discovered it was governed by the largest tribe in Ethiopia, which had recently gained power through democratic means, ousting a smaller tribe that had held control for years. This political shift sparked a civil war, primarily concentrated in the northern region of the country. However, danger seemed to loom everywhere. For instance, during my visit to the Red Museum, which documented the brutal reign of terror by the Communists in Ethiopia, riots erupted within the Muslim community, resulting in the museum being set ablaze. Whether it was enduring rolling blackouts or facing water shortages, you never really knew what to expect from day to day.

Once I settled into the college, my classes began. I found myself surrounded by eager pastors hungry to hear the Word of God taught. Among them was a remarkable individual who had escaped from Eretria, a Communist country to the north, where he had been imprisoned for his faith. After completing my class and securing his degree, he intended to return clandestinely to his homeland to preach and teach God's word.

Another student of mine was embarking on a perilous mission to evangelize in Somalia, a venture fraught with danger. It is estimated that for every ten Somalis we reach for Jesus, Muslim extremists kill nine. Tragically, the cultivation of church leadership in Somalia is hindered as potential leaders are often targeted and murdered before the work gains momentum.

I count it as an extraordinary privilege to have been entrusted with the opportunity to dedicate my time and resources to teach these Ethiopian students. Thank you, Jesus, for this privilege!

Inwardly, I wanted to preach in these pastors' churches, but I've never asked anyone if I could preach in his church. I assumed if God wanted me there, he would open the door without me asking. "A man's gift makes room for him and brings him before great men" (Proverbs 18:16). However, at the time, I failed to grasp the significance of the honor-shame culture prevalent across the African continent. The pastors hesitated to directly request my preaching services, fearing potential rejection and subsequent public humiliation. Consequently, we found ourselves at an impasse until one pastor ingeniously devised a plan to broach the subject with me.

This pastor approached the missionary hosting me, requesting that he inquire if I would be interested in preaching. This indirect approach provided him with a safeguard in case of potential rejection. However, I had no intention of declining the invitation; I was genuinely thrilled by the opportunity. When news spread around the Bible College that I eagerly accepted the offer to speak at the church, all the pastors lined up to request me to preach. Suddenly, doors throughout the entire country were opened to me. Unfortunately, due to my limited visa and plane tickets, I couldn't reach them all.

After completing my teaching assignment and preaching, I returned to Springfield, Missouri. During that time, Global University was hosting a meeting with our Distance offices from various parts of the world. Dr. Seevers graciously extended me the opportunity to address these international leaders. With fervor, I delivered my message and poured out my heart to the audience.

Following the session, a Colombian gentleman named Juan Rodriguez approached me. He expressed how deeply my message had resonated with him. Juan, along with his brothers and father, had played pivotal roles in establishing the church Avivamiento in Bogota, Colombia, which boasts approximately 100,000 members.

Pastor Rodriguez approached me and said, "Alex, I would like to extend an invitation for you to minister within the prison system of Colombia. If you're willing, you can preach to Communist guerrillas." For years, I had been reading about the Communist insurgents known as the FARC. Though a peace treaty had been signed by the Colombian government with the FARC several years ago, many of its members remain incarcerated today. Pastor Rodriguez possessed both the influence and the willingness to facilitate my entry into ministering to these men. Without hesitation, I accepted his offer.

Around this time, I managed to rent a house for Crystal and me. This charming little cottage nestled on the side of an Ozark Mountain outside Springfield, near a quaint town called Clever. I informed my parole officer about our impending move. He then explained that my relocation would necessitate a transfer to another parole office, given the change in geographical location. Consequently, I would be assigned a new parole officer to oversee my case. This news was particularly disheartening.

Upon receiving a transfer notice, I was instructed to report immediately to a parole officer in the city of Nixa. Upon arrival, I introduced myself and explained my circumstances. However, she regarded me skeptically. I laid out all the documentation I had gathered, including the necessary paperwork for my upcoming trip to Bogota, Colombia. She examined the documents uncomfortably before stating, "I can't grant you permission to travel. I'll need to contact Louisiana and inquire if they will allow you to travel."

I tried to reason with her, emphasizing that travel was an integral aspect of my job. I likened it to a carpenter being deprived of their hammer—how would he make a living? This work is my means of paying rent; without it, how would I survive?

She responded coldly, "That's not my problem," and promptly dismissed me, indicating that our meeting was concluded. With a dismissive gesture, she turned her back on me, adding that she would contact me once Louisiana provided a response. Feeling dejected, I walked away, knowing all too well the prevailing attitudes of Louisiana bureaucrats towards ex-prisoners. My immediate future now rested in the hands of an embittered public servant who likely believed I belonged at McDonald's flipping burgers with other former convicts.

Several days passed since that disheartening encounter. As the departure date for my flight to Colombia drew near, the phone finally rang, and the name of the new parole officer flashed across the screen.

I answered politely, "Hello, Ma'am," but received a blunt response in return: "Louisiana called and said that you could not travel anywhere."

Shocked by this news, I attempted to revisit my reasoning about the necessity of traveling for work and the importance of paying bills. This was my livelihood! However, she reiterated, "That's not my problem." In a somewhat ironic twist, she reminded me not to forget to pay my parole fee for her oversight. Each month, individuals on parole are required to pay approximately $50 to the parole department to maintain their freedom. It was a bitter irony that she was essentially obstructing my employment while simultaneously reminding me to pay the State of Missouri.

Feeling dreadful, I reached out to Pastor Rodriguez to explain that both the State of Missouri and Louisiana had deemed it in the best interest of Louisiana citizens for me not to travel to Bogota, Colombia, to reach out to the Communist guerrillas with the message of Jesus. Following our conversation, I started contacting those who had offered assistance during previous crises. Mrs. Graham and Mrs. Brandes swiftly mobilized their networks, prompting the involvement of several politicians and the staff at Global University.

I received news from a highly influential source indicating that the Louisiana Parole Board had received a motion to consider allowing me to travel for employment purposes. Essentially, the board would convene to make an administrative decision regarding whether I could travel with their permission. This decision would also dictate who would oversee my case. If granted permission to travel, my parole officer would be expected to comply with the board's ruling, regardless of any changes in leadership within the parole department, both in Louisiana and Missouri. This decision would remain unaffected by shifts in governing philosophy. However, if the board ruled against my travel, it would effectively bring my career to an abrupt halt.

A couple of weeks after receiving this information, I had to visit my parole officer again. As I entered her office, she quickly retrieved some paperwork that had been forwarded to her. Without much preamble, she informed me that I was now permitted to travel anywhere for work, provided I obtained a pass. To my immense relief and joy, the Louisiana Parole Board had ruled in my favor. With this decision, I could now move forward and accept the ministry opportunities that came my way.

To my surprise, Dr. Wayne Cook, the gentleman I worked for during my prison missionary trip, contacted me. He had relocated to Guadalajara, Mexico, intending to retire. However, instead of retiring, he found himself accepting the pastorate of the largest Presbyterian church in the area. It seemed ministry was something he couldn't let go of. Alongside his pastoral duties, he initiated the Lakeside Theological Institute, aiming to provide theological training in Chapala. During our conversation, it felt as though we were back in the Louisiana prison system. Without hesitation, I gladly accepted his invitation to teach a course, conduct a seminar, and deliver a sermon to his congregation.

Upon my arrival, I was greeted by the Church's humble staff and immediately immersed myself in the work at hand. During a service, I shared my testimony, and the Spirit of God moved profoundly, touching the hearts of those present. Families graciously opened their homes to me, eager to delve deeper into the Word of God, so I conducted teachings in homes across the city. Additionally, we launched their inaugural class on Prison Ministry. Among the attendees was a remarkable woman who had endured unjust incarceration in a Mexican prison for eight years. Despite the hardships she faced during her imprisonment, she ultimately proved her innocence and regained her freedom. However, the toll of her experience on her health was evident. Nevertheless, she harbored a fervent desire to support women currently incarcerated in Mexico.

The class went exceptionally well, and I also conducted a seminar on Transforming the Criminal Mind. Among the attendees were several Baptist pastors, who showed keen interest in the discussions. Dr. Cook's church ran a benevolence ministry that provided food to these pastors and their congregations. Engaging in conversation with them, Dr. Cook proposed the idea of me preaching in their churches, to which I enthusiastically agreed. During one of these services, a man seated near the front listened intently to my sermon. As I spoke, he began trembling and shedding tears. Sensing a divine prompting, I approached him and embraced him. He wept on my shoulder for several minutes, deeply moved by the message.

After he regained his composure, he stood before the congregation and made a confession in Spanish. My interpreter conveyed to me that he had just renounced his ties to drugs and the Cartel. He declared his readiness to lay down his life for Jesus. The weight of his words didn't fully sink in until later. In America, it's common to hear people profess their willingness to die for Jesus, but the true cost of Christianity often isn't felt there (at least not yet). Such declarations are rarely put to the test to gauge sincerity. However, a missionary once remarked to me that without God's intervention, the Cartel would likely have killed him. Oh, my Lord and Savior, may the body of Christ in America come to experience and embrace such fervent love and commitment to Jesus before their faith is put to the ultimate test.

Upon my return to America and settling back into my office, I was greeted by an unexpected email from Gaborone, Botswana. The director of the nation's sole accredited Bible College had previously extended an invitation for me to teach their inaugural Masters' students. The Assembly of God Bible College had a track record of successfully graduating students at the Associate and Bachelor levels. Now, they were aspiring to attain national accreditation for their first Master's program. In response to their request, I agreed to teach a Hermeneutics class and promptly submitted my transcripts for approval by the Botswanan government. Fortunately, my application was swiftly approved, and we wasted no time in finalizing the dates for my class.

In order to accept this trip to Botswana, Africa, I would be responsible for my plane tickets, lodging, and food. The Lord had taken care of my trips to Ethiopia and Mexico, and I knew He would provide for this opportunity to serve as well. Ironically, just as I was contemplating this, the phone rang, and it was a pastor's wife from New Jersey. She was trying to reach me on behalf of her husband, Pastor John James, who felt led to invite me to New Jersey to speak at their Mission's conference. Without hesitation, I agreed. I could sense her pleasant surprise. I assured her of my commitment to supporting the local church, which I believe serves as the conscience of our nation. Speaking to God's people in the church is one of my greatest honors.

This amazing church was founded in Paterson, New Jersey, under the direct influence of William J. Seymour, who led the Azusa Street Revival. Eventually, the church became part of the Assemblies of God and relocated to Wyckoff, New Jersey. They generously flew me to New Jersey and granted me the opportunity to address both their leadership and the Missions Conference in separate services. The Holy Spirit moved among us, touching lives and leading people to surrender to the Lord. I watched in awe as the Lord drew His people closer to Him. As the service concluded and I was preparing to leave, the pastor handed me an envelope, which I tucked into my jacket pocket. Upon reaching my hotel, I opened the envelope to find a check inside. It covered all my expenses for the trip to Botswana. Once again, God had provided.

Soon, I found myself boarding another plane bound for Africa. Opting to save a few dollars, I chose to fly into Johannesburg, South Africa, and then use an African airline to reach Botswana. Initially, I hadn't given much thought to this decision. However, as I neared South Africa, I couldn't help but wonder if I would be sharing the plane with chickens, goats, or even terrorists. Eventually, I made a conscious effort to push aside these negative thoughts and replace them with a positive perspective: I appreciated animals, and what a remarkable opportunity it would be to lead a terrorist to the Lord! With this mindset, I experienced an enjoyable flight and arrived in the capital, Gaborone, right on schedule.

My classroom was brimming with a diverse array of individuals: pastors alongside professionals from the secular realm—a military colonel, a government Minister of Finance, lawyers, schoolteachers, and businessmen. Each participant possessed a keen eagerness to absorb and understand the Word of God. It was an extraordinary blend of people, each offering valuable insights into their country. While I imparted their first course in Hermeneutics, I, in turn, received a crash course in Botswana. Interestingly, Botswana stands out on the continent for its prevalence in the practice and teaching of witchcraft. I later discovered that some church members frequently engaged with witch doctors due to their deep entrenchment in the local culture.

Livestock freely roamed the streets. I asked my guide what kept the animals from being stolen or eaten. He explained that everyone takes their livestock to the witchdoctor to perform a curse over them so that anyone who eats the meat without paying for it comes under the curse. Unfortunately, when some church people get sick, they often turn to the witchdoctor before seeking medical help. I witnessed this disturbing reality firsthand when I was invited to preach in the local church. As I delivered the sermon, the Spirit of God began moving across the congregation. However, when I called upon people to surrender their lives to Jesus, demons started manifesting.

Some of the women in the congregation came forward to be freed from the spirits that plagued them with vile thoughts. I placed my hands on these precious women's heads and commanded the spirits to leave them in Jesus' name. Some crumpled into the chairs behind them, while others stood and wept as the spiritual weight lifted from them. This experience would challenge the theology of many of my friends. However, it is closer to the reality of the New Testament we all read than the lectures we often hear in our seminaries and on podcasts.

Once I arrived back in the United States, I had a conversation with Mrs. Ruth Graham. During our discussion, I mentioned to her that I still possessed the handwritten promissory note from Mrs. Mary Brandes, which guaranteed to bring me to the Cayman Islands to minister with her and her husband. Mrs. Brandes had given me this note along with her contact information while I was in prison. Mrs. Graham advised me, "Hold on to it, and one day you can redeem it." I cherished it like a precious treasure, connecting my faith to its promise. I confidently declared, "One day, I will turn in this ticket for real." After my conversation with Mrs. Graham concluded, she reached out to Mrs. Brandes and explained that I had held onto the ticket in faith, and that I still possessed it.

After that conversation, my phone rang. It was Mrs. Mary. She was planning a ministry trip to the Cayman Islands and wanted to know if I was available. She intended to have Commissioner Cain's Prison Seminaries Foundation, the prison authorities from Grand Cayman, and me sit at a table to discuss the possibilities of establishing a seminary inside the prison on Grand Isle. The core idea was to utilize Global University's curriculum to train inmates for ministry work within the prison. This trip came to fruition, and I found myself at the table with those mentioned. We concluded the meeting with a positive outlook, foreseeing that this school could soon become a reality. Before we left the facilities, I was offered the opportunity to preach to the inmate population, and I eagerly accepted.

Mrs. Brandes had also invited Mrs. Graham and a Baptist pastor from Grand Cayman to participate in the service. Mrs. Graham and I had engaged with the pastor's congregation the day prior. That evening, as we were checked into the Main complex and escorted to the prison chapel, the Spirit of God was palpable among the prison population. When the guards announced the commencement of the church service, half of the prison population opted to attend. Perplexed, the guards couldn't comprehend the sudden surge of interest in the gathering. They suspected it might be indicative of a potential escape attempt or brewing riot, prompting the prison staff to remain on high alert.

Once everyone from our group was introduced to the inmate population, I was handed the microphone to preach. Sharing my story, I felt the Spirit of God begin to move among these men, stirring hearts with conviction. As the service drew to a close, I offered an altar call for those who wished to repent and accept Jesus as their Lord. Remarkably, over three quarters of the men present stepped forward to surrender their lives to Jesus. The response was overwhelming; so many men crowded the front of the chapel that I couldn't reach them all to lay my hands on them. Resorting to standing on the pews, I began to walk down them, reaching out to each man as best I could.

The service was a resounding success, prompting Mrs. Brandes to engage with several influential families and government officials. Together, they generously offered us the Civic Center on Cayman Brac at no cost for an evangelistic event. This initiative marked a significant shift as none of the churches on Cayman Brac had collaborated in such a manner before. The Spirit of God evidently moved among the men and women, compelling them to unite in their efforts to reach out to the community. Through collective endeavors, everyone pitched in to advertise, set up chairs, manage sound equipment, and warmly greet attendees.

While en route to Cayman Brac for this event, I received an important call. Mrs. Brandes informed me that I had been approved to speak at the high school to all the 9th, 10th, 11th, and 12th-grade students. Upon arrival, as we made our way through the school, I entered an auditorium packed with every high school student on Cayman Brac. I approached them with the same urgency I would offer to lost souls in dire need of salvation. The Spirit of God moved among them, reminiscent of my experiences in prison. During the altar call, half of the students chose to surrender their lives to the Lord. On that day, they embraced Jesus as the Lord of their lives.

Following that, I delivered a sermon at the Civic Center, with all the churches collaborating to ensure its success. I thought this marked a fantastic conclusion to an extraordinary trip, but then the phone rang once more. Mrs. Brandes asked if I would be willing to preach at an open-air event. Despite never having done so before, I agreed without hesitation. The plan was to erect a small wooden stage in front of the bars and deliver the sermon from there, with folding chairs scattered across the parking lot. As night fell, the atmosphere crackled with anticipation. Once again, all the churches came together to support this event, undoubtedly shifting the atmosphere in our favor. Before the night ended, we had filled all the chairs, with others listening from their cars.

It was truly an amazing way to conclude the trip!

Upon my return to Springfield, I found a message from Warden Darrel Vannoy awaiting me. He had assumed the role of head warden at Wilkinson County Correctional Center in Mississippi, a facility notorious for housing the state's most violent and dangerous inmates under Maximum Security lockdown, identifiable by their red and white striped attire. Aware of the spiritual revival that transpired in the Cayman Islands, Warden Vannoy extended a succinct invitation: "Want to come preach to these guys?" With my immediate supervisor absent, I reported directly to Dr. Seevers. Explaining the invitation and its potential impact, I received his unwavering support without hesitation. He offered his blessing and urged me to proceed. I embarked on the approximately nine-hour journey to Wilkinson County, Mississippi, securing a hotel room upon arrival.

The following day, as I pulled into the parking lot, Warden Vannoy greeted me warmly, opening the prison gates and ushering me through with a reverence akin to royalty. He navigated me past all the security checkpoints, dismissing officers as if I were a dignitary, perhaps even the governor or his own kin. In a departure from conventional penological practices, Warden Vannoy brought together rival gangs under one roof for a church service, defying the usual segregation. Before me sat members of the Latin Kings, Vice Lords, Gangster Disciples, Simon City Royals, Aryan Brotherhood, Crips, and the Bloods. With just a brief introduction, a microphone was placed in my hand. I felt in my heart that something divine was about to unfold. As I began to speak, I sensed the Spirit of God moving through me.

When I issued the altar call, over three quarters of the men present responded by stepping forward to be born again and accept Jesus as their Lord and Savior. As they gathered at the front of the room, I closed my eyes and offered worship to God. Upon opening my eyes, I witnessed these men huddled together, holding hands with heads bowed and eyes closed. Guiding them in prayer, we collectively repented of our sins and embraced Jesus as Lord. Together, we surrendered our lives and committed to follow Jesus, each shouldering our own crosses. As we concluded with "amen," those men departed forever changed. It was indeed a profound privilege to preach to these men!

During this period, I had been collaborating with Pastor Ray Bradbury, a distance student in Buenos Aires, Argentina, who was pursuing his doctorate. Pastor Bradbury, a dedicated missionary, had devoted twenty years of his life to serving in the capital city of Argentina. He felt a divine prompting to invite me to South America to impart teachings that had profoundly impacted him. Without hesitation, I accepted the invitation. However, the bureaucratic protocols of my university position required numerous signatures to formalize the trip. Moreover, arranging travel expenses including plane tickets, accommodation, and meals was essential. Once again, I found myself in need of a financial miracle.

In the interim, Pastor Tino Cione from Lanham, Maryland reached out to me. We had crossed paths at the Georgia event, where he had obtained my contact details. Pastor Tino possessed an athletic build, a ready smile, and a relaxed demeanor that endeared him to everyone he met. Upon recognizing him, I felt an immediate surge of positive emotions. I greeted him with a cheerful, "What's up?" To which he responded, "How do you feel about coming up here for a couple of weeks and preaching?" Excitedly, I replied, "I'd love to." He then informed me, "Good, I talked to President Severs, and he cleared you to come." His words sparked laughter from me.

I packed my bags in preparation for my trip to the East Coast. Upon landing at Baltimore airport, Pastor Tino was there to greet me. Initially, I had anticipated speaking at three or four services during my visit, as per the initial invitation for a couple of weeks. However, to my surprise, I found myself preaching every day and twice on Sundays throughout Maryland and Virginia. Witnessing people flocking to the altars was truly remarkable; it was evident that God was at work in a special way. Amidst our whirlwind schedule of visiting different churches, Pastor Tino mentioned the possibility of speaking at a high school. True to his word, he arranged for me to speak at Lanham Christian School. I approached these students with the same passion, recognizing their desperate need for a savior.

One of the most impactful moments of the trip occurred when Pastor Tino proposed that I preach to the group of illegal immigrants whom Texas Governor Abbott had recently dropped off in Washington, D.C. Just months prior to my visit, Governor Abbott had faced an influx of illegal immigrants into Texas. In an act of political frustration, he arranged for buses to transport them to Washington, D.C., and Martha's

Vineyard, where they were left. Recognizing the evident need, Pastor Tino responded by facilitating the establishment of a Spanish-speaking church led by a pastor within a section of his facilities. Within a remarkably short span of time, this initiative led to the birth of a new church community among these immigrants. Now, I was presented with the opportunity to minister to them.

Following Pastor Tino's morning service, the congregation of Central and South American individuals convened for their own church gathering on the same premises. As I made my way towards their meeting area, the resonating sounds of Spanish worship filled the air. Stepping into their service, I seamlessly joined their worship experience. Eventually, the Spanish pastor introduced me to the congregation and entrusted me with the microphone. With fervor, I poured out my heart to them, issuing a passionate call to repentance and faith. The Holy Spirit moved powerfully among the adults first, prompting many to kneel in surrender at the altar, their tears a testimony of their encounter with God. Sensing the depth of the moment, I relinquished the microphone to the pastor and retreated to the side of the stage, humbly stepping aside to allow God's work to unfold unhindered.

The pastor felt led to call the young people next. This prompted the second wave of the Spirit. As the youth came forward, they began falling to their knees and weeping tears of repentance. God was embracing this group of people with love and forgiveness. I stood by, watching with tears in my eyes.

Toward the end of my Maryland visit, Pastor Tino asked me about my upcoming schedule. I mentioned the invitation to Argentina. He expressed his desire to inform the church during the next service and provide them with an opportunity to support me financially. The following service held two surprises for me. Firstly, the Spirit of God was palpably present, leading people to surrender their lives to the Lord. Then, Pastor Cione announced my invitation to Argentina. Suddenly, a spirit of generosity swept through the congregation, and individuals began giving beyond their tithes to facilitate my trip. I was deeply moved by their generosity as they covered my travel expenses, lodging, and meals.

When Pastor Tino handed me a check before I left, I was overcome with a sense of reverence and awe for the gift. I recognized that what I held in my hands was sacred. Before my departure, Pastor Cione did one more thing that deeply humbled me. He expressed his desire to take me out and purchase a nice suit. Indeed, he accompanied me to a shop where I was fitted for two tailored suits!

The second surprise in Maryland came in the form of a nineteen-year-old businessman from El Salvador, Guillermo Enrique Bardales Romero, who preferred to be called Enrique. This remarkable young man was not only a millionaire but also displayed borderline genius. His early life was marked by adversity as his family had to hide him across El Salvador from the notorious gang MS-13 during his first decade. His mother, seeking a better life in the U.S., sent money back home to support the family, drawing the gang's attention due to the new clothes Enrique wore. Faced with threats from MS-13 demanding regular payments or her son's life, his family moved him across the country with the help of a network of relatives.

When his mother was finally able, she called for Enrique to join her in Maryland. Over the next five years, he immersed himself in the culture and language of America. It was during this time that he realized the boundless opportunities available in the country—he could achieve anything and become anyone he desired. With unwavering determination, Enrique set his sights on becoming a wealthy businessman.

From the ages of fifteen to nineteen, Enrique established seven companies and acquired numerous rental properties. Additionally, he invented a Solar umbrella, patented the design, and developed a method for easy installation in rural areas, providing power access. Notably, he was also set to become the son-in-law of the associate pastor, James Boyce. As I was departing the service, Pastor Boyce requested a moment to speak with this remarkable young man.

At that moment, I didn't know his background or who he was. I listened intently to what he had to say: "Dr. Hennis, I would like to fly you to El Salvador to preach the gospel. I want to donate a Solar umbrella to a rural village that has no power. I want to give them light, but I want you to give them the gospel light." I didn't need a burning bush or an angel to appear to confirm that I needed to do this with him. I knew in my heart that this was God opening another door of opportunity.

After we exchanged information, Pastor Boyce took me to the airport to catch my flight back to Springfield, Missouri. Once I returned to the office, I was able to get the necessary approvals for my trip to Argentina. Pastor Bradbury had an extensive itinerary planned across the capital and the province. The day of departure arrived. My flight had a short layover in Peru. In a few hours, I boarded another plane and headed across the Andes Mountains to my destination. Shortly before my arrival in Buenos Aires, a couple of million people were protesting in the streets against the Socialist government and the massive inflation they created. This protest was happening downtown right where I would be staying.

Fortunately, the crowd had dispersed before I landed. Crystal texted me to inquire if I was okay. I responded, "Yes, the crowd has gone." To my surprise, she replied, "What do you mean? I'm talking about the massive earthquake that happened in Peru!" Just after my plane took off, the earthquake occurred. I didn't realize then the providential hand of God was guiding me through unseen dangers. Undoubtedly, the safest and most beneficial place a Christian can be is walking in faith and obedience to God's will for their life. Ultimately, God can be trusted to lead us where we need to be.

Pastor Bradbury picked me up at the airport and escorted me to my accommodations. Soon after, we embarked on a journey across Argentina, attending various meetings together. As I delivered my sermons, the Spirit of God would stir within the congregation, drawing individuals closer to Jesus. Across multiple churches, the altars filled with men and women surrendering their hearts to the Lord. Furthermore, God showcased His power by touching hearts, liberating them from bitterness and unforgiveness. His love permeated through His people in profound new ways, refreshing them and igniting a fervent passion for the Lord.

During a particularly significant gathering, Pastor Bradbury introduced me to Ben Grahams. Mr. Grahams' grandfather, a missionary, had acquired the former Nazi headquarters in Buenos Aires after World War II, transforming it into a Bible College. Over time, the responsibility for the college passed to his son, and now Ben, the grandson, assumed leadership of Biblico de la Plata. Today, Ben graciously provided me with an opportunity to address the Bible College students, who would go on to become Argentina's future Christian leaders. I recognized that by positively influencing these emerging leaders, I could indirectly impact all those who would later heed their guidance.

I poured out my heart to these young believers, and soon the Spirit of God began to move among them. Witnessing their fervent response, they approached the altar, falling to their knees in surrender. Tears streamed down their faces as they prayed passionately, craving more of God's presence. The chapel resonated with the fire of God as His spirit swept through, igniting hearts. We worshipped in this manner until a profound sense of reverence enveloped us. After composing ourselves and concluding the service, the students quietly departed for their next class, deeply impacted by the encounter.

As Pastor Ray and I were departing, Mr. Grahams handed me an envelope containing pesos. Initially, I felt compelled to decline the money and return it to him, as I had come to Argentina with the intention of giving rather than receiving. However, in that moment, the significance of giving resonated within me. I recalled the biblical accounts of various widows' offerings, recognizing the connection between sacrifice, giving, and blessings. Understanding the importance of supporting such an esteemed institution in a politically and economically challenging environment, I accepted the gift and offered a prayer over it. It felt as though I was holding a treasure from heaven in my hands.

As it was time to bid farewell to Argentina, I expressed my gratitude and bid goodbye to Pastor Bradbury and his family. He kindly dropped me off at the airport, and soon I was en route back to the United States. Upon my return to Springfield, I delved into organizing the logistics for my upcoming trip to El Salvador. Despite my efforts, official clearance through the expected channels proved challenging, as I was unknown to the individuals associated with Global University in El Salvador, who had been working there for years. While they weren't resistant, the political climate and cultural sensitivity necessitated that I travel independently, rather than being affiliated with them or the university. In essence, I found myself navigating this journey alone.

Enrique had arranged the airline tickets and preceded me to El Salvador to make preparations for the event. Upon my arrival at El Salvador's International Airport, I was warmly welcomed by a representative from Enrique's team and escorted to a black SUV waiting outside. We made our way to the capitol building, where I soon found myself seated across from the governor of the state, Ever Salinas, at the Oficina Uicn El Salvador. Enrique was also present, elucidating the details of our outreach efforts to the political leadership. After he concluded, Governor Salinas expressed his enthusiastic support, stating, "I love what you guys are doing. You have my complete backing. Anything you need, please let me know." His endorsement was resolute, as he promptly contacted the media to announce the event, even deciding to broadcast it across Central America, showcasing his unwavering support for our initiative.

Shortly after our meeting, Governor Salinas attended a gathering with President Nayib Bukele and other governors from across the country. During this assembly, Governor Salinas briefed everyone on our outreach efforts and the potential benefits for the people of El Salvador. Shortly thereafter, all the governors approached Enrique, expressing their interest in having us conduct similar initiatives in their respective states. Suddenly, I realized that the entire country of El Salvador had just opened its doors to me.

Meanwhile, a work crew transported the materials to the site where they planned to assemble the Solar umbrella and formally present it to the people. I would also deliver a sermon there once the village gathered together. Unfortunately, a severe storm struck the area and washed away the mountain road that provided access to the village. All work had to be halted. As the rain fell and lightning streaked across the sky, I cried out to God to cease the storm and enable us to reach the top of that mountain. Eventually, the rain subsided, and Enrique contacted the governor to explain the situation.

After the call, Governor Salinas assured us that he would dispatch heavy equipment into the mountains to carve a road to the village. He pledged that we would reach the mountaintop in time for the sermon. Time was of the essence as my flight was scheduled to depart the following evening. Through the grace of God, the road was swiftly cleared to the village, and the Solar umbrella was successfully assembled. Everyone, including the governor and members of the media, gathered eagerly to hear my sermon and witness the formal presentation of the Solar gift. Glancing at my watch, I realized that immediately after the sermon, I needed to depart the mountain promptly to catch my flight. Time was running short.

After I delivered an evangelistic sermon, Enrique briefed the governor about my urgent need to reach the airport swiftly. Governor Salinas quickly made arrangements and provided me with a police escort off the mountain, racing across San Salvador at approximately 80 miles per hour. Upon arrival at the airport, the police officers promptly took charge of my bags and escorted me to the front of the line, ensuring I was swiftly checked in for my flight. They then guided me through customs and escorted me directly to the terminal where my plane awaited. With a firm handshake, one of the officers said, "Dr. Hennis, thank you for ministering to the people of El Salvador. Have a safe flight." With a smile, he turned and departed. Moments later, as my plane soared into the sky, I settled into my seat, overwhelmed with gratitude, and whispered, "Thank you, Lord, for this extraordinary experience."

Once back home, Crystal and I resumed our search for a church to join. Despite visiting various churches and engaging with different communities for several months, we hadn't found the right fit yet. Ironically, during this time, Pastor Carl Everett, who was vacationing in Missouri, expressed a desire to introduce me to a pastor friend of his who lived near me. While Crystal was visiting her family back in Mississippi, I attended the worship service alone. Upon my arrival, Pastor Carl introduced me to Pastor Ben Davis of Abundant Life Church, and an instant connection was forged.

Pastor Ben had organized an outreach in San Pedro Sula, Honduras, scheduled for a couple of months later. When Pastor Carl introduced me, he referred to me as his spiritual son. This introduction held significant weight for Pastor Ben, who regarded it as sufficient to grant me ministerial standing in his eyes. Essentially, Pastor Carl extended to me a considerable amount of credibility based on his reputation and the longstanding relationship they shared. If I could afford the tickets and lodging, Pastor Ben welcomed me to join his team. Without hesitation, I expressed my eagerness to participate.

When Crystal returned from Mississippi, I excitedly shared with her that I had found a church for us. Initially, she seemed a bit hesitant. However, during the first service we attended together, Pastor Ben called on both of us to join the prayer team for the altar call. This gesture of inclusion in their service deeply resonated with Crystal and me. In that moment, we felt assured that we had discovered a place where we could serve and cultivate meaningful relationships with fellow believers.

Pastor Ben swiftly recognized my spiritual gifts and started incorporating me into the teaching and preaching rotation for the

Honduras trip. Our itinerary included ministering at a conference attended by over 400 Foursquare pastors and conducting outreaches at various churches across the country. Additionally, we planned to engage in street evangelism targeting specific sections of cities. To bolster our efforts, Pastor Ben decided to accompany us with a medical team, providing free healthcare services to those in need.

During this time, I received a text from Pastor Charlie Tuttle at Genesis Church in McKinney, Texas. He decided to open the door and allow me to speak to his church. I gladly agreed to the date and time. Upon my arrival, he had booked a nice hotel for me and fed me like a king. When the day finally arrived, I shared my story with his church and the people responded by filling the altar. We had a blessed time worshiping God together. As the service ended and I was preparing to leave, Pastor Tuttle asked me for some contact information. He was planning to electronically transfer some funds to me.

I provided him with the information and then headed back to Missouri. Throughout our time together, I never disclosed any of my needs or the financial challenges looming ahead. Upon arriving at my driveway, I noticed a notification on my phone from Pastor Tuttle. Opening the email, I discovered that he had provided enough funds to cover my expenses in Honduras. Once again, God had come through!

Soon, I found myself on a plane bound for Central America. As soon as the plane touched down in San Pedro Sula, we boarded a bus headed to our inaugural church service. Although Pastor Ben was slated to deliver the sermon, he desired to involve all of us with vocal gifts in the service. Towards the conclusion of his message, he beckoned me onto the stage, handing me the microphone and instructing me to conclude the sermon. With fervor, I delivered a heartfelt plea for individuals to surrender their lives to the Lord. Witnessing a response, people began leaving their seats and streaming towards the altar. The prayer team accompanying us swiftly sprang into action. It was remarkable to witness the work of God as the team laid their hands on these precious individuals and offered prayers.

Throughout the trip, Pastor Ben continued to empower and utilize me. At two pastor's conferences, he allocated an hour each time for me to minister to the assembled men and women. Following my sermons, I witnessed the Spirit of God profoundly impacting these pastors, reigniting their fervor and zeal. It was moving to see their dedication, with some having walked or ridden bicycles for miles to attend the conference, while others relied on rides from fellow believers. Some even scrimped and saved to afford public transportation to be present. Our hearts were intertwined with theirs as God poured out His Spirit upon those in attendance. It was an extraordinary way to impact the country by uplifting its Christian leaders.

After the conferences, we embarked on a journey to a mountainous region of the country. I was teamed up with a translator named Danny, a young woman in her twenties. Alongside us was a guide, a woman well into her sixties. Initially, I had a fleeting concern about the older woman's stamina, but she quickly proved me wrong. This grandmother displayed the spirit of a lion and the endurance of a long-distance runner. She quietly warned us that the area was controlled by the drug cartel.

Surprisingly, rather than fear, I felt a surge of excitement. What better place to carry out street evangelism?

As we traversed the streets, I would pause to engage people in conversations about the gospel and the importance of having a savior. We even took the initiative to knock on doors, and were graciously welcomed into homes, allowing entire families to hear the gospel message. Upon leading someone to make a decision to accept Jesus as their Lord and Savior, our seasoned guide would step in to collect their contact information for follow-up ministry and to connect them with her church. This approach proved to be remarkably effective.

As we continued walking, my guide veered onto a stone trail leading into the mountains, and I followed obediently. Soon, we found ourselves ascending the mountain via well-trodden paths. Perched along the cliff sides were houses, nestled into the rugged terrain. At each one, we made our presence known, announcing ourselves. Eventually, a resident would emerge, graciously inviting us inside. Sometimes, even before I uttered a word, the Spirit of God would descend upon the household, evoking tears from those within. The palpable presence of God was undeniable. It seemed as though the Lord was drawing these individuals to Himself even before I had the chance to speak.

Sweating profusely, we persevered through the sweltering jungle heat, pushing onward along the trails. My seasoned guide glanced up at the towering mountain ahead and unleashed a roar in Spanish. Curious, I turned to my interpreter and inquired about her words. Danny relayed, "She said there isn't sufficient daylight remaining for us to proceed. She's frustrated and determined to conquer the entire mountain for Jesus!" Reflecting silently, I couldn't help but think, "I wish my fellow believers back in America shared the same level of concern and fervor for reaching their communities for Jesus."

After safely returning from our trek, Pastor Ben's team came together with the local church, and we organized a children's outreach complete with games and prizes. All the street evangelism and walking were also aimed at advertising the service that night. Prior to arriving in Honduras, we packed our suitcases full of balls, candy, glow sticks, coloring books, and toys. I chuckled at the contrast of once smuggling drugs across borders to now trafficking toys and candy for children. By the time the service arrived, I found myself surrounded by hundreds of children. That night, we played games, performed a skit, and preached the gospel. The response was incredible. These precious children were praying to receive Jesus as their Lord and Savior. The church workers who were present helped organize them into the church by collecting the parents' contact information. What an amazing conclusion to our trip!

Once back in the United States, I received a text from Scott Holmes, who happened to be in Springfield, MO. I thought it would be a great idea to connect with him and introduce him to Crystal. We arranged to meet at a popular local ice cream shop. During our conversation, he mentioned his upcoming trip to Mozambique, Africa. The Louisiana District's leadership was planning an official outreach in the capital city. Intrigued by the prospect and having heard of some challenges there, I expressed interest in joining the trip.

When I expressed my interest in joining, Pastor Scott enthusiastically welcomed me, saying, and "Come on." With my immediate supervisor at the university on vacation, I approached Dr. Gary Severs for permission to partner with the Louisiana District and accompany them on the trip. He replied, "Alex, if your work is caught up here, you have my permission to go." I assured him that it was. Subsequently, I found myself included in Zoom calls with both the Louisiana District's leadership and the missionary couple who would be hosting us, Toby and Melinda Magill. Given Toby and Melinda's awareness of the potential dangers ahead, they would oversee this mission. With me included, there would be ten men and two women working on this project.

Our plan was to fly into Johannesburg, South Africa, hire a bus, and embark on a roughly seven-hour journey crossing the border into Mozambique. Upon arrival in Maputo, the capital, our itinerary included various activities such as working on the missionary couple's compound, constructing a church structure for a local community, visiting the country's oldest Bible College, and conducting church outreaches. Despite the potential hardships and challenges ahead, we deemed them insignificant compared to the opportunities we had to serve the Lord.

By now, you can almost anticipate what the Lord is about to do. Shortly after that phone call, I opened my work email and found an invitation from Pastor Andy Parks of Cross Point Church in Paola, Kansas. He had invited me to preach to his congregation. I gladly accepted and made the trip to Kansas. His church was brimming with believers who had a deep love for Jesus. However, like most, they also had loved ones who were not walking with the Lord. After sharing my testimony, I felt compelled to invite the congregation to come forward to the altar and stand in the gap for those loved ones who needed to hear the message but weren't present. Before long, the altar was filled with people.

We engaged in an intense session of interceding with the Lord for the salvation of these individuals. After pouring out our hearts, a sense of comfort and assurance swept across the sanctuary. People were uplifted and infused with fresh confidence that the Lord was in control of their loved ones' destinies. As I was preparing to depart, Pastor Parks summoned me to his office. He wanted to write me a check as a gift. Little did he know, his generosity would help offset the costs of my trip to Mozambique, Africa.

Upon returning to Springfield, I began diligently filling out paperwork and obtaining the necessary documents for my upcoming trip. Additionally, I delved into studying the culture and history of Mozambique. I discovered that in 2020, Muslim extremists had invaded the northern section of the country, prompting Rwanda's military to assist Mozambique in expelling the terrorists. Prior to this invasion, Mozambique had been plagued by years of civil war instigated by Marxists, which nearly tore the country apart. Nevertheless, despite these challenges, my heart remained steadfast in its commitment to ministering to these people.

In due time, I boarded a plane, and sixteen hours and twenty-two minutes later, it touched down in Johannesburg, South Africa. A bus awaited us, ready to pick us up. We embarked on a seven-hour drive until we reached the border separating South Africa and Mozambique. There, we unloaded and walked across the border, going through customs procedures. Once again, we boarded the bus and continued our journey to Maputo. Upon arrival at Toby and Melinda's compound, we immediately got to work: welding, cutting steel beams, grinding, and painting.

The following day, we journeyed to a nearby community and began unloading the steel beams, tin sheets, and tools required to construct a tabernacle. Given the consistent warm temperatures, all that was necessary for a church structure was steel beams supporting a tin roof. With the concrete foundation laid the previous day, we erected the steel beams, secured them with bolts, and interconnected them with joists. Subsequently, we affixed the tin sheets onto the frame to form a robust roof. In just about eleven hours, our team of twelve had completed the construction of a church. Throughout the day, the community had steadily gathered to observe our progress. Once our task was accomplished, everyone congregated beneath the newly built church's roof for an impromptu service. We sang hymns, offered prayers, shared words of dedication, and preached the gospel.

Sunburned and jet-lagged, we embarked on our journey the following day to the country's oldest Bible College, where we were greeted by the directors. It struck me with irony that despite its esteemed history, the school was currently striving for national accreditation and required additional qualified professors to support its ambitious goals. Aware of the challenges faced by pastors in the war-torn northern regions of the country, it was clear to me that many couldn't afford the journey south for training. Even if they managed to overcome the financial barriers, there was no guarantee that their churches would still stand upon their return.

I proposed the idea of sending electronic equipment to the missionaries stationed in the north, enabling them to receive classes remotely from the Bible College. This initiative would establish extension centers where northern pastors could access training. Additionally, I offered to return and teach at the school, viewing this endeavor as a remarkable opportunity to contribute to the discipleship of the nation.

The suggestion resonated positively with everyone present. Louisiana leaders promptly drafted a list detailing the required equipment and recommended fundraising efforts upon our return to the U.S.

The director of the Bible College also served as the National Missions director for the Assemblies of God churches in Mozambique. In addition to these responsibilities, he was the pastor of a four-hundred-member church. The following morning, I was invited to minister to his congregation. Every chair was occupied, with many individuals standing along the church's sides. As he introduced me and handed over the microphone, I could feel the presence of God. After delivering the sermon, I issued an altar call for individuals to surrender their lives to

Jesus. The Spirit drew men and women nearer to Him, and soon the altar was filled with about one hundred people.

After concluding the service, the pastor embraced me, declaring that what we had witnessed was the early flames of revival. He expressed his eagerness for my return to teach at the Bible College, assuring me that his church doors would always be open. The elders of the church came forward, enveloping me in a Capulana, a traditional African garment. Nobody, myself included, seemed to be in a rush to depart. It was awe-inspiring and humbling to witness the work of the Lord unfold. Regrettably, our time was limited. We soon boarded the bus and made our way back to South Africa to catch our plane.

Upon arriving at O.R. Tambo International Airport, we boarded our plane for the lengthy journey back to the United States. Upon touchdown, Crystal was there to pick me up. During each of my trips, I made an effort to find a special gift to bring back for her. Over time, I realized that she cherished a simple coffee cup more than fancy jewelry. She enjoys drinking her coffee from a different cup each day, so she happily adds the new cup to her collection. In contrast, I stick to my trusty Yeti cup every day.

For the first seven years while she waited for me to be released, I thought we were so similar that we might have been twins separated at birth. However, after getting married, I've come to realize that two people could not be more different from each other. At times, all I can do is laugh at this reality. Nevertheless, I want the world to know that she is a divine gift who continually inspires me to pursue integrity, especially when nobody else is watching.

Upon returning to the office, I received a text from Pastor Carl Everett, asking if I would be interested in taking his place on a ministry trip to Cuba with a group from Family Life Church in Lafayette, Louisiana. His leg was bothering him at the time, so he didn't feel up to making the trip. The plan was to minister inside the house churches scattered across Havana. Additionally, we would partner with a house church and engage in street evangelism and preaching throughout the capital. I felt honored to step in for Pastor Carl and thrilled at the opportunity to preach the gospel in Communist Cuba.

Up until now, I've been fully immersed in my work, finding so much enjoyment in it that I never saw fit to take a day off or utilize any accumulated vacation time. It's somewhat embarrassing to confess, but I wasn't even aware that I had vacation time to begin with. Perhaps HR mentioned it when I first joined, but it slipped my mind. After all, my previous line of work involved no such perks as vacation days or 401K plans. Recently, my supervisor brought to my attention that I had accrued a significant amount of unused vacation time, and warned me that if I didn't take some time off, I'd lose it.

I made the decision to embark on my first vacation. Therefore, when completing my travel documents, I designated myself as a tourist. I flew to Louisiana where I met up with the team from Lafayette, comprised of four men and four women. After introductions, we boarded a plane in New Orleans and approximately five hours later, we touched down in Havana, Cuba. Upon arrival, we were greeted by a pastor who would serve as our guide, leading us through the various house churches scattered across the capital city. To facilitate our travels, we had arranged to rent a bus for the trip, ensuring smooth transportation for the entire team.

One of the initial churches we visited was an apartment where several walls had been removed to form one spacious room. The couple resided in a small room, with the remainder of the apartment serving as a place of worship. As we engaged in worship through song, the Spirit of God permeated the congregation in an extraordinary manner. Individuals responded to the presence of the Lord with tears, and profound expressions of repentance were voiced as both men and women dropped to their knees. This profound experience continued for several hours.

After boarding the bus, we returned for the night to the Airbnb accommodations we had rented. Early the following morning, we set off for the next ministry site. This particular house church featured a spacious courtyard with a roof serving as its sanctuary. It was here that I shared my testimony and witnessed the Lord stirring the hearts of the attendees, instilling them with hope. Ministering to these individuals evoked memories of the prison environment I had previously encountered. Despite having limited resources and restricted freedom of expression, they exhibited remarkable resilience, making the most of what they had and worshiping God with genuine exuberance.

The following morning, we visited another house church characterized by dirt floors and a tin roof supported by poles in the front yard. The folding chairs were assorted and mismatched, with some metal chairs showing signs of rust. Despite the modest surroundings, the Cuban congregants arrived dressed in their finest attire, demonstrating their reverence for the King who sacrificed Himself on the cross for their salvation. The music portion of the service extended for about an hour. Subsequently, each member of our team shared segments of their testimony. Attendees eagerly approached the altar, seeking prayer from us. Their fervent desire to encounter God in a deeper way was palpable.

That same evening, I was tasked with delivering a sermon at a sizable house church in downtown Havana. The pastor expressed deep gratitude for the opportunity to host a guest speaker from the United States. I shared my heartfelt message with the congregation, and as the service concluded, individuals began approaching the front spontaneously, without any formal invitation. Wave after wave of people stepped forward, seeking prayer or making a decision to surrender their lives to Jesus. Amidst this powerful moment, I heard some women cry out from the other side of the church.

Looking across the room, I witnessed a remarkable moment: a young boy with cerebral palsy took his first unassisted steps. (His parents later confirmed this to us.) The church members erupted in screams, shouts, and praises, overwhelmed by the awe-inspiring sight. We continued to worship through song for at least an hour following this extraordinary miracle. Interestingly, God became the focal point in the aftermath of this display of power. In other words, no individual received credit for this miracle; it was clearly attributed to God. I believe this is the way it should always be.

Regrettably, as our time dwindled, we weren't able to engage in door-to-door and street evangelism. Our team had to pack up and make our way back to the airport. Before long, we were airborne, bound for the U.S. Upon my arrival stateside, Pastor Ben Davis reached out to me. He extended an invitation for me to return to Cuba if I was interested in participating in door-to-door and street evangelism. He mentioned that he was sending three individuals to Cuba through the same connections that I had just experienced.

With plenty of unused vacation time at my disposal, I made a firm commitment to embark on this second trip. Nearly two weeks later, I found myself flying back to Cuba. Upon landing, we were shuttled to our Airbnb accommodations. Interestingly, another American group opted to join us in this endeavor, significantly boosting our numbers. The following day, I was dropped off at one of the churches where I had previously preached. The church members were eager and committed to walking alongside me through the streets of Havana as I shared my faith.

I was paired with an interpreter and a local guide for support. As we strolled through downtown, I took the lead in guiding people to make the decision to accept Jesus as their Lord and Savior. I engaged in conversations with construction workers, delivery personnel, young individuals, entertainers, and various colorful characters. A dedicated church member accompanied us at all times, collecting their contact information for follow-up ministry and integration into the local house church. Together, we marched through the streets of Havana, boldly sharing the message of Jesus, firmly believing that the Lord's power transcended the confines of the Communist government.

By the following day, we had led over one hundred and fifty individuals to accept the Lord. These newfound believers joyfully gathered with us at the beach to partake in baptismal ceremonies in the ocean. It was a truly awe-inspiring sight to witness so many people publicly proclaiming their newfound faith in Jesus. Following this profound experience, I chose to retreat to my Airbnb, where I could focus and complete the final lines of this book.

As fate would have it, I find myself seated in the very area of Havana, Cuba where Ernest Hemingway penned "The Old Man and the Sea." What an inspiring setting to conclude sharing my testimony! For years, I've harbored the desire to write my story, yet I could never muster the resolve to sit down and begin. It dawned on me one day that I was still living out unwritten pages. Thankfully, I invested in a laptop and carried it with me across the globe. Over the past year, I've finally begun to put my story into words. It's not merely about the transformation of Angola, or my liberation from prison, or my remarkable role at the university. It's about realizing the vision that God bestowed upon me over a quarter of a century ago in that prison cell. The final chapter of this book recounts my journey to preach the gospel throughout the world.

Always remember these words of encouragement: nothing can deter a praying individual with a God-given vision burning within their heart. In my earlier years, as a boxer, I endured three amateur rounds, each lasting three minutes. I quickly realized that victory wasn't solely determined by skill. Instead, it went to the fighter who relentlessly pressed forward, and did not stop punching. Essentially, success didn't hinge on appearance or agility but on perseverance until the final bell rang. Our journey with God mirrors this truth. Amid challenging times, I urge my students: keep pressing forward! When faced with difficulties in ministry and work, I remind my colleagues: keep pressing forward! The Apostle Paul's words resonate: "And let us not be weary in well doing: for in due season we shall reap, if we faint not" (Galatians 6:9). If you distill my story into a life lesson, it would be this: God can use a failure in life, but He cannot use a quitter. He can transform your mess into a message. So, don't relent—keep punching!

Made in United States
Orlando, FL
13 May 2024

46824245R00108